LEANLINE COOKERY

HILDA WOOLF

LEANLINE COOKERY

100 low calorie recipes metricated by the
Good Housekeeping Institute

EBURY PRESS
LONDON

Published by Ebury Press
National Magazine House
72 Broadwick Street
London W1V 2BP

First impression 1979

ISBN 0 85223 146 6

Editor Barbara Argles
Designer Derek Morrison
Line drawings by Pat Robson
Colour photography by Philip Dowell

Jacket photograph shows
Courgettes with leeks (page 85), Rosy chicken (page 77),
'Leanline' baked potato halves (page 86),
Raspberry whip (page 100)

The author and publisher would like to thank the following
for their help in providing props:
David Mellor (jacket photograph),
Liberty & Co. Ltd (photograph facing page 45).

Filmset and printed in Great Britain by
BAS Printers Limited, Over Wallop, Hampshire
and bound by
Cambridge University Press Limited, Cambridge

For Madeleine

Acknowledgments

Mr H. J. Leal, Principal of Eltham Adult Education Institute, London SE9, and Mrs F. Lawes, Tutor in charge at Gordon School, gave their unfailing support and enthusiasm for an innovatory project. The students who consistently participated in my 'Leanline' classes, many staying on for a second and third year, showed a keen appreciation of good food which has been inspiring. I offer my sincere thanks to all these people.

I should also like to thank Mrs Helen Gomme for testing recipes and her family for enjoying them.

I should like to express special thanks to my family, for their zealous encouragement as well as critical comments. In particular, to my husband, Dr P. Grahame Woolf, for his perceptive appraisal of the draft text.

Contents

Introduction

Having covered the gourmet cookery scene for some years, it had become increasingly apparent to me that there was an urgent need for a complete reappraisal of modern cookery in terms of health and well-being for *everyone*.

Seven years ago I initiated a slimming and health cookery course at The Eltham Adult Education Institute (ILEA). Housewives with responsibility for keeping their families fit, recently retired people and students wishing to remain slim forcibly endorsed by own belief that food should always be a pleasurable and satisfying experience. People obliged to eat *less* food, deserve the best.

This was the beginning of my 'Leanline' cookery. I set myself the absorbing task of creating dishes which anyone would enjoy, whether slimming or not. They were tried out at home and tested in class. My approach has been to create a lighter style of low calorie cookery which highlights the true flavours of food. It is low in fats, starches and sugars and high in protein, in line with expert opinion on health and fitness. Nor is it expensive, as several high cost ingredients, such as heavy cream and fats, are reduced to a minimum or replaced entirely by aromatic marinades and natural juices of fruit and vegetables. A certain amount of fibre or 'roughage' is included and small amounts of wholemeal flour, bran and bran products are incorporated into the recipes. Gradually, tastebuds are re-educated, so that the natural flavour of food is fully appreciated and this, in turn, encourages people to reconsider their eating habits.

'Leanline' cookery is for the novice as well as the experienced gourmet cook. The recipes do not involve time-consuming preparation; they are practical and lead towards a pleasurable 'Leanline' lifestyle.

Hilda Woolf

A note about calories

All foods are potentially fattening. If your food intake is more than you use up in terms of energy, the surplus will be converted into fat.

It is essential to measure the amount of food you eat, and calorie counting remains the most helpful method of calculation.

However, very few foods have a stable composition, and therefore slight discrepancies are encountered between values given in different publications.

Where appropriate, recipes have been rounded up and down to the nearest 5 or 10 calories.

My principal source of reference has been McCance and Widdowson's 'The Composition of Foods', revised edition by A. A. Paul and A. T. Southgate (HMSO 1978).

I have also consulted:

MINISTRY OF AGRICULTURE, FISHERIES AND FOOD
THE MILK MARKETING BOARD
TATE & LYLE REFINERIES LIMITED
ROCHE PRODUCTS LIMITED
FLOUR ADVISORY BUREAU
MARKS & SPENCER LIMITED
U.S. DEPARTMENT OF AGRICULTURE

Useful calorie counts

FRUIT
per 100 g (4 oz)

apples *40*
apricots *25*
  stewed without sugar *20*
bananas, flesh only *80*
  weighed with skin *47*
blackberries *29*
blackcurrants *28*
gooseberries, green *17*
  stewed without sugar *14*
grapefruit, whole *11*

grapes, black *61*
  white *63*
lemons, whole *15*
  juice *negligible*
melons, Canteloupe with skin *15*
  yellow, Honeydew with skin *13*
oranges, whole, *26*
  juice, fresh, per 100 ml (4 fl oz) *38*

peaches, whole *32*
pears, whole *29*
pineapple, fresh *46*
227-g (8-oz) can pineapple slices
  in natural juice *133*
  432-g (15¼-oz) *246*
raspberries *25*
rhubarb *6*
strawberries *26*
tangerines *34*

DRIED FRUIT
per 25 g (1 oz)

apricots *45*
  stewed without sugar *16*
currants 60

dates, stoneless *62*
figs *53*
  stewed without sugar *30*

prunes, with stones *33*
  stewed without sugar *18*
raisins *62*
sultanas *62*

VEGETABLES
per 100 g (4 oz) unless otherwise stated

aubergines *14*

avocado pear, flesh only, per 25 g (1 oz) (depending on type and ripeness) *25–55*

broad beans, boiled *48*

French beans, boiled *7*

runner beans, boiled *19*

bean sprouts, raw *32*
   canned *9*

beetroot, raw *28*
   boiled *44*

broccoli, boiled *18*

Brussels sprouts, raw *26*
   boiled *18*

cabbage, white and red *20*

carrots *20*

cauliflower, raw *13*
   boiled *9*

celeriac *14*

celery *8*

chicory *9*

courgettes *12*

cucumber *10*

Jerusalem artichokes *18*

leeks *24*

mushrooms *13*

onions, raw *23*
   boiled *13*

parsnips *56*

peas, fresh, boiled *52*
   frozen, boiled *41*

peppers *15*

potatoes, new, boiled *76*
   jacket-baked *85*

spinach *30*

spring greens *10*

swedes *18*

sweetcorn, canned kernels *76*

tomatoes, fresh *14*
   canned *12*

paste, per 15 ml (1 level tbsp) *20*

FISH
per 100 g (4 oz)

cod, raw, fillets *76*
   frozen steaks *68*
   smoked, poached *101*

haddock, fresh, raw *73*
   smoked *101*

kipper, with bones *111*

mackerel, raw *223*
   smoked *240*

plaice *91*

prawns *107*

trout, whole *89*

tuna, canned in oil *289*
   drained of oil *236*

MEAT
per 100 g (4 oz)

beef, lean, raw *123*
   mince *229*
   rump steak grilled, lean only *168*

lamb, lean, raw *162*

leg roast, lean only *191*

liver *179*

pork, lean, raw *147*
   leg roast, lean only *185*

POULTRY
per 100 g (4 oz)

chicken, roast, meat only *148*
   meat and skin *216*
   boiled, meat only *183*

turkey, roast, meat only *140*
   meat and skin *171*

MISCELLANEOUS INGREDIENTS USED IN 'LEANLINE COOKERY'
per 25 g (1 oz) unless otherwise stated

flour, wholemeal (100%) *80*

rice, raw *90*
   boiled *30*

spaghetti, raw *96*
   boiled *30*

All-bran *69*

gelatine, 1 envelope *33*

cream, single, per 25 ml (1 fl oz) *62*

whipping, per 25 ml (1 fl oz) *103*

soured, per 25 ml (1 fl oz) *54*

skimmed milk, per 600 ml (1 pint) *190*

natural yogurt, per 150 ml (5 oz) (see 'Leanline' recipe) *60*

cottage cheese *30*

curd cheese *34*

butter *226*

low fat spread *105*

corn oil *260*

sunflower oil *250*

stock cubes (Knorr) *30*

orange juice, reconstituted frozen, per 150 ml (¼ pint) *60*

grapefruit juice, reconstituted frozen, per 150 ml (¼ pint) *55*

tomato juice, per 100 ml (4 fl oz) *16*

red wine, per 100 ml (4 fl oz) *68*

white wine dry, per 100 ml (4 fl oz) *66*

Useful information for 'Leanline' cooks

CONVERSION TO METRIC MEASUREMENTS

The metric measures in this book are based on a 25 g unit instead of the ounce (28.35 g). Slight adjustments to this basic conversion standard were necessary in some recipes to achieve satisfactory cooking results.

If you want to convert your own recipes from imperial to metric, we suggest you use the same 25 g unit, and use 600 ml in place of 1 pint, with the British Standard 5-ml and 15-ml spoons replacing the old variable teaspoons and table-spoons. These adaptations will sometimes give a slightly smaller recipe quantity and may require a shorter cooking time.

Note Sets of British Standard metric measuring spoons are available in the following sizes – 2.5 ml, 5 ml, 10 ml and 15 ml.

When measuring milk it is more convenient to use the exact conversion of 568 ml (1 pint).

For more general reference, the following tables will be helpful.

METRIC CONVERSION SCALE

	LIQUID				SOLID	
Imperial	*Exact conversion*	*Recommended ml*		*Imperial*	*Exact conversion*	*Recommended g*
¼ pint	142 ml	150 ml		1 oz	28.35 g	25 g
½ pint	284 ml	300 ml		2 oz	56.7 g	50 g
1 pint	568 ml	600 ml		4 oz	113.4 g	100 g
1½ pints	851 ml	900 ml		8 oz	226.8 g	225 g
1¾ pints	992 ml	1 litre		12 oz	340.2 g	325 g
				14 oz	397.0 g	400 g
				16 oz (1 lb)	453.6 g	450 g

For quantities of 1¾ pints and over, litres and fractions of a litre have been used.

1 kilogram (kg) equals 2.2 lb

Note Follow either the metric or the imperial measures in the recipes as they are not interchangeable.

OVEN TEMPERATURE CHART

°C	°F	*Gas mark*
110	225	¼
130	250	½
140	275	1
150	300	2
170	325	3
180	350	4
190	375	5
200	400	6
220	425	7
230	450	8
240	475	9

Equipment

Elaborate equipment is not required for 'Leanline' cookery. The pieces listed, correctly used, will give life-long service. I find them indispensable.

Pepper mill To obtain the true flavour of pepper.

Kitchen scissors For cutting, snipping and trimming, especially fish and poultry.

Knives Razor-sharp, for carving, chopping or slicing.
A chef's knife is the most useful all-purpose shape. My own favourite is a Swiss stainless steel knife which sharpens easily.
A small, serrated-edge paring knife, again in stainless steel, is invaluable for slicing vegetables and fruits.
A vegetable peeler ensures that minimum peel is removed.
A grapefruit knife for scooping flesh from fruit and vegetables.
A palette knife is useful for countless cooking tasks.

Kitchen scales Must be accurate.
Perforated long-handled spoon

Food mills
The mouli-julienne will shred and slice raw vegetables. It has five cutting discs and is probably my most over-worked gadget. The *mouli-legumes* will purée soups, vegetables and all cooked mixtures.
The blender is invaluable. Pounding, puréeing and grinding take seconds. Plastic goblets may retain spicy aromas so whirl cold water mixed with a little vinegar for a few seconds to ensure an odour-free blender.

Pestle and mortar Perfect for pounding the hard spices like coriander, cardamom, cumin, whole peppercorns, etc, as well as garlic and herbs. Otherwise, improvise with a small flat-bottomed basin and the end of a rolling pin.

Pots and pans
The 'Leanline' method of cooking food with the absolute minimum of fat (sometimes none at all) necessitates the use of *heavy-based pans*. A wide, shallow saucepan is preferable to a small deep one, so that the food to be cooked is quickly in contact with the source of heat. An enamel-lined, cast-iron casserole is a sound investment. It can be used over a flame or in the oven, so eliminates transferring food from one pan to another. 5 ml (1 tsp) oil is used to protect the lining and prevent scorching of certain ingredients. An overnight soaking in mild detergent effectively removes stains.
Non-stick pans are often disappointing. The pan itself must be of high quality, thick and robust, to stand up to long term fatless cooking. It is usually necessary to brush the surface with oil. However, heavy based aluminium pans are excellent for 'Leanline' cookery and my ancient collection has withstood the various techniques described in this book.

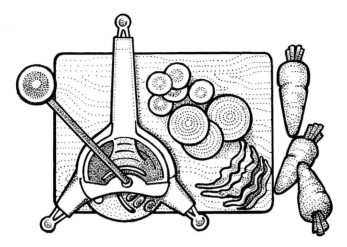

A mouli-julienne – used for shredding and slicing raw vegetables

Ovenproof dishes, glass, enamel-lined or stainless.
A large china bowl or dish with a non-corrosive lining is essential for marinating ingredients.

Flavourings

I am convinced that many people ignore everyday store cupboard ingredients because they have not explored their potential. Cinnamon, nutmeg, mixed spice, ginger and cloves are used in my recipes. Worcestershire, soy, tabasco and tomato-based sauces all have their place. English and French mustards, smooth or grainy, wine and cider vinegars, horseradish relish as well as freshly grated raw horseradish, help to flavour dishes and dressings.

Pepper and salt
I use freshly ground black pepper all the time. If you don't own a mill it is still worth using whole black peppercorns for marinades and other dishes, as indicated in the recipes. Sweet paprika pepper, preferably Hungarian, is worth seeking. I prefer real salt as opposed to the refined pouring salt. Buy a packet of sea salt or coarse salt and keep it for salads, dressings and bread. The difference in taste is remarkable.

Spices
Other spices include juniper berries, coriander seeds, cardamom pods, cumin and ground turmeric. Whole spices retain their aroma much more effectively than ground. It is most important, therefore, only to buy small quantities of ground spices and to store them in airtight containers.

Herbs

Fresh herbs are always an asset, but are not easily available.

Finely chopped fresh parsley stores in the refrigerator for several days. Parsley sprigs freeze well, and stalks should also be frozen and used to flavour home made stocks.

Fresh mint is undervalued and insufficiently used. It is worth freezing. Certain dried herbs add interest and variety to food. Again, it is essential to buy in small quantities, from a shop with a fast turnover, and to store them in a cupboard away from the light. Any dried herb with a dusty appearance must be stale and not worth buying.

Garlic

Garlic, peeled and crushed in salt, dissolves into the cooking liquid with pleasing results. A little fresh garlic improves dressings, stuffings etc.

Vanilla

The true vanilla flavour is only obtained by using a vanilla pod. Stored in an airtight jar it will keep for months. Use it, wash in warm water, *dry thoroughly* and store. A cut pod, buried in a jar of sugar or fruit sugar, will impart its delicate aroma to the sugar.

Orange and lemon peel

Use only the zest as the white pith is bitter. A potato or vegetable peeler easily removes the essential peel.

The cost of these flavourings is modest: their aromas add great variety and character to food.

Other ingredients

Fats

Fats, being a source of concentrated energy, contain more calories an ounce than any other food. The advantage of oil is that the exact amount required can easily be measured. Sunflower-seed and corn oil are useful all-purpose oils. They are high in polyunsaturated fats and recommended for anyone on a cholesterol lowering diet. I love good butter. A surprisingly small amount is enough to enhance the flavour of vegetables, soups and fish.

Low fat spread is extremely useful, especially in cakes, as it offers large calorie savings. It is best used straight from the refrigerator. Try mixing it with butter for choux pastry.

Cottage and curd cheese

Cottage cheese soaks up flavours in a most accommodating way. Mixed with yogurt, it replaces the fat element in many 'Leanline' recipes.

Curd cheese, low to medium fat, has a smooth texture and interesting flavour, with a calorie count similar to cottage cheese. It is particularly suitable for cheesecake and is a good base for a variety of herbs and other ingredients which transform it into excellent light cheese starters or spreads. It is available from supermarkets and delicatessens.

Skimmed milk

Liquid skimmed bottled milk is invaluable. Unopened, it will keep in the refrigerator for several weeks. Opened, it has a longer refrigerator life than fresh milk, and half the calories. I find the taste less obtrusive than dried skimmed milk powder and have used it wherever milk is indicated in a recipe. However, dried skimmed milk powder is a useful store-cupboard ingredient and can successfully replace whole milk. I like it, too, as a thickener when making yogurt (see Yogurt).

Cream

Single cream, soured cream and, occasionally, whipping cream are suggested as worthwhile alternatives to double cream.

Lemon juice

Heavy dressings are unnecessary when fresh, subtle-tasting vegetables are available. Savour the true taste of salads. A sprinkling of fresh lemon juice adds a refreshing element to raw or cooked vegetables. Store lemons in the refrigerator. Bottled lemon juice is used in countless ways in 'Leanline' cookery. Keep it in the refrigerator, tightly capped.

Yogurt

Yogurt is an essential ingredient of 'Leanline' cookery. It helps to flavour and tenderise meat, poultry and fish; it replaces the oil in marinades; it thickens and smooths sauces and adds interest to vegetables. Yogurt absorbs flavours so it is ideal as a base for all types of herbs, spices and seasonings. The permutations for interesting salad dressings are endless. Mixed with hot summer or autumn fruits it makes a most refreshing dessert. In many of my recipes it replaces double cream to excellent effect.

There was a time when I bought my yogurt, because making it seemed rather a hit and miss affair. However, as my yogurt consumption grew I sought a reliable, uncomplicated method, using skimmed milk. My choice was the Deva Bridge Yogurt Maker, unbelievably easy and absolutely foolproof. Of course, you can use an insulex jar instead. The addition of 15 g ($\frac{1}{2}$ oz) dried skimmed milk powder produces a thick creamy yogurt.

You will need 5 ml (1 tsp) fresh yogurt as a 'starter'. Put it into the insulated jar. Measure 15 g ($\frac{1}{2}$ oz) dried skimmed milk powder into a jug and stir in 30 ml (2 tbsp) from the 568 ml (1 pint) cold skimmed liquid milk, making sure it is smooth. Mix in the remainder of the milk. Pour into a saucepan and bring gently to the boil. Remove from heat and cool to 49°C (120°F). Stir a little of the cooled milk into the yogurt and gradually add the rest. This will lower the temperature to 43°C (110°F). Cover the jar with the inner and outer lids and leave for 5 hours to set. Then store, covered with the inner lid, in the refrigerator. It will keep for a week. Use 5 ml (1 tsp) of this yogurt for your next batch. I make a point of cleaning the jar thoroughly each time, with plenty of hot water only – **no detergent**. To refresh the yogurt, start occasionally with 5 ml (1 tsp) of the commercial variety. You now have a low price, low fat, low calorie supply of creamy yogurt.

235 calories per 600 ml (1 pint)

Sweetening agents

Saccharin (artificial sweetener) is the only zero-calorie sweetener available. Many people find its flavour acceptable in drinks but less so in food. It is unsuitable for cooking as heating intensifies the bitter taste. Therefore, it has to be added at the end of the cooking period and in the smallest possible amount.

Fructose or fruit sugar *106 calories per 25 g (1 oz)*
Fructose is a natural sugar occurring in almost all sweet fruits and berries. One half of the dry substance of honey consists of fructose. Although it has a calorie-count similar to ordinary sugar, it is considerably sweeter.

Fructose enhances the flavour of food, especially fruits of every type. Its greatest asset, however, is that it will successfully mask the unpleasant bitter after-taste and 'mouth feel' of saccharin. A sweetening mixture of fructose and saccharin is indistinguishable from sugar, as demonstrated in 'Leanline' recipes, with calorie savings of up to 80 per cent. In my cake recipes I have combined fructose and sugar with excellent results. Although more expensive than sugar, a small amount, usually 15 g ($\frac{1}{2}$ oz), is all that is needed when a recipe requires sweetening. Fructose is available from health food stores and chemists. Eventually it is sure to become more widely available.

Sugar
I have indicated small quantities of caster sugar or brown sugar where either is essential to a recipe.

Natural sweetening
Wherever possible, I use both dried and fresh fruits for sweetening. Ripe bananas, fresh pineapple and pineapple canned in natural juice are all immensely sweet. Dried fruits such as prunes and apricots, pre-soaked and cooked for a short-time, are reasonable in calories and contain dietary fibre (roughage).

Dates *62 calories per 25 g (1 oz)* These are intensely sweet. Finely chopped or coarsely ground dates actually resemble certain types of brown sugar both in taste and appearance. This date 'sugar' is lower in calories than honey and is not a refined carbohydrate. It is extremely valuable in cakes, adding bulk and flavour as well as sweetness. Buy the stoned packet dates. They are inexpensive and perfectly satisfactory for cooking.

Treacle Black treacle has a distinctive flavour. A teaspoonful will enhance a fruit purée or add interest to a cake. Again, it is lower in calories than sugar or honey (*64 calories per 25 g (1 oz)*) is certainly useful and deserves a place in the store-cupboard.

Stocks and soups

Home made stock makes an incredible difference to the flavour of soups, sauces, stews and casseroles. All fish dishes are improved immensely when real fish stock is used.

Never throw away the carcass of roast poultry; try the chicken and turkey stocks in this section. Save fresh poultry bones and trimmings and store them in a polythene bag in the freezer until it is convenient for you to make stock. Freeze it in 300-ml and 600-ml ($\frac{1}{2}$- and 1-pint) containers.

Butchers will sell fresh beef and veal bones very cheaply. Have them chopped into manageable pieces, then freeze them in polythene bags as for poultry bones until you want to use them.

People resist making fish stock. It sounds troublesome. In fact, like other stocks, it takes very little time to prepare. Fish stock does require fresh fish bones and trimmings, so it means shopping and cooking on the same day.

Once you have acquired the stock-making habit, you will use the commercial kind for emergencies only.

An important element is that the calorie content is negligible.

Soups

Home made soup must surely be one of the most economical foods available and is always a success. A hot vegetable soup, thick or thin, makes a satisfying beginning to any meal. Made more robust with the addition of cheese and toasted croûtons, or crisp vegetable garnishes, it is an ideal lunch, high tea or light supper dish.

Soups can be stored covered in a refrigerator for up to 4 days. It is a good idea to freeze soups in different size containers, so that the required number of helpings may be easily available. Thawing and reheating must be gentle. Always check the seasoning before serving.

When preparing soups, if butter is necessary use no more than 15 g ($\frac{1}{2}$ oz), which is melted over a low heat. The vegetables are cooked or 'sweated' in hot butter, with the lid on the pan, to extract the maximum flavour. An alternative method leaves out all fat and uses stock alone for cooking. This is particularly suitable for anyone on a special diet.

All soup recipes may be halved or doubled in quantity. Once you have acquired the 'Leanline' soup-making habit you will rarely turn to the canned or dried varieties.

Fish stock

If you have saved any fennel stalks and leaves, this is the time to use them. Otherwise, use 5 ml (1 level tsp) dried fennel seeds.

1 leek
strip of lemon peel
1 bay leaf
6 whole peppercorns
6 coriander seeds
a few parsley stalks
2–3 chopped fennel stalks and about 15 ml (1 tbsp) feathery leaves or

2.5–5 ml ($\frac{1}{2}$–1 level tsp) dried fennel seeds
1 clove garlic, skinned
5 ml (1 level tsp) salt
1 carrot, peeled and thinly sliced
1 onion, skinned and thinly sliced
700–900 g ($1\frac{1}{2}$–2 lb) fish bones, heads, skin, trimmings etc

Trim the leek. Cut off the dark green stalk and slice the remainder thinly. Wash thoroughly in plenty of cold, lightly salted water until you are certain that every particle of grit is removed.

Place the prepared leek in a large saucepan with all the seasonings and other vegetables. Break up the fish bones if necessary and add them to the pan. Cover with cold water, partially cover the pan and bring slowly to simmering point. Skim and simmer, with the lid tilted, for 40 minutes. Strain through a nylon sieve and cool completely. Cover and store in the refrigerator for not more than 2 days.

Freezing note Freeze in 300-ml ($\frac{1}{2}$-pint) containers. Suitable quantities will then be readily available for cooking fish or making sauce.

Calories are negligible

Turkey stock

This clear stock is extremely useful for adding flavour to stews, casseroles, soups and gravy. It is rather lightly salted and seasoned so that it will blend admirably with a large variety of dishes.

1 turkey carcass
1 large onion, skinned and quartered
2 sticks celery with leaves, washed and chopped
1 medium carrot, peeled and quartered
5 ml (1 level tsp) salt
sprig of parsley and a few extra stalks
1 clove garlic, skinned

1 bay leaf
a strip of lemon peel
1.25 ml ($\frac{1}{4}$ level tsp) dried thyme
10 whole peppercorns
10 coriander seeds
2.5-cm (1-in) cinnamon stick or 1.25 ml ($\frac{1}{4}$ tsp) powder
seeds of a cardamom pod

Scrape away any stuffing from inside the carcass. Break the carcass into pieces and place in a very large saucepan. Add the prepared vegetables. Pour in sufficient cold water to cover. Add the salt and bring slowly to the boil, uncovered. Remove any scum which rises to the surface and then add all the seasonings. Partially cover the pan with a lid and simmer gently for 2 hours.

Strain the stock into a large bowl, pressing all the juices from the bones and vegetables with the back of a large spoon. Cool uncovered. Pour into suitable containers and leave in the refrigerator until the fat has set in a layer on top of the stock so that it can easily be removed.

This stock can either be frozen and used as required or stored in the refrigerator, covered, for up to 3 days.

Cleared of all fat, this turkey stock contains negligible calories

Chicken stock

This stock is made with the carcass of a roasted chicken and, if available, one or two extra giblets from the freezer – not the livers. It is one of my most useful freezer standbys and is guaranteed to transform any soup, sauce or stew into first class fare!

1 roasted chicken carcass
175 g (6 oz) onions, skinned and
    quartered
2 medium carrots, peeled and
    quartered
2 sticks celery with leaves, washed
    and chopped
sprig of parsley and a few extra
    stalks

1 clove garlic, skinned
about 3 litres (5–6 pints) water
1 bay leaf
strip of lemon peel
5 ml (1 level tsp) salt
12 whole black peppercorns or 1.25 ml
    ($\frac{1}{4}$ level tsp) powder

Scrape away any stuffing from inside the carcass. Break the carcass into six pieces. Use the browned skin but discard the parson's nose and any fatty pale pieces of skin. Put all the bones, skin and vegetables into a large saucepan and pour in sufficient cold water to cover. Bring to the boil, uncovered, over a moderate heat. Remove the scum which will rise to the surface as boiling point is reached. Add the bay leaf, lemon peel and seasoning. Reduce the heat, partially cover the pan and simmer the stock for $1\frac{1}{4}$ hours.

Drain through a colander into a large bowl and cool, uncovered, preferably in a larder, never in a warm kitchen. Any residual fat will rise to the surface and can easily be spooned off. Pour into suitable containers. Freeze or store in the refrigerator, covered, for up to 3 days.

Cleared of all fat, this chicken stock contains negligible calories

Turkey giblet stock

turkey giblets (heart, gizzard and
  neck)
1 small turnip, peeled
1 small carrot, peeled
1 small onion, skinned
1 clove garlic, skinned
1 bay leaf

1 stick celery with leaves, washed
a few parsley stalks
1.25 ml ($\frac{1}{4}$ level tsp) dried thyme
5 ml (1 level tsp) salt
6 whole peppercorns
900 ml–1.1 litres ($1\frac{1}{2}$–2 pints) cold
  water

Wash the turkey liver and pat dry on kitchen paper. Set aside for use in a stuffing or gravy.

Soak the giblets in cold salted water for 1 hour. Drain and put them in a saucepan with all the other ingredients. Add cold water to cover. Partially cover with a lid and bring to the boil over moderate heat. Reduce the heat and simmer gently for 1 hour.

Strain the stock into a bowl and cool, uncovered. Leave in a refrigerator and remove the fat when it has formed a thin layer on the surface. Freeze or store in the refrigerator for up to 3 days.

Note The cooked giblet meat may be chopped and added to clear soup.

Calories for turkey stock cleared of all fat are negligible

Celeriac soup

Celeriac is one of my favourite vegetables; it has a deliciously nutty flavour and is particularly good raw with a mustardy yogurt dressing. It is cheap, keeps very well in the refrigerator and provides the basis for a really nourishing soup. At long last, it is becoming more widely available; if you have difficulty in finding a supply, try nagging your green-grocer.

1.1 litres (2 pints) home made chicken
  stock or make up using 1 chicken
  stock cube
450 g (1 lb) celeriac, before peeling
10 ml (2 tsp) vinegar or lemon juice
175 g (6 oz) onion

100 g (4 oz) carrot
5 ml (1 level tsp) salt
8 twists of pepper from a mill or good
  pinch powder
1 bay leaf

Heat the stock to boiling and leave on one side while preparing the vegetables. Peel the celeriac and leave in cold water containing 10 ml (2 tsp) vinegar or lemon juice. Peel the onion and carrot and, if possible, coarsely grate the three vegetables together or chop into small pieces. Put all the vegetables in the hot stock, season and add the bay leaf. Cover and simmer for 30 minutes.

Cool and purée all but a cupful of the soup. The combination of purée plus some of the vegetable pieces adds interest and texture to the final soup. Reheat and adjust the seasoning. If liked, add a 7-g ($\frac{1}{4}$-oz) pat of butter to each bowl of soup just before serving.

Freeze or store in the refrigerator, covered, for up to 3 days.

Serves 6

25 calories per serving
80 calories per serving (with butter)

Jerusalem artichoke soup

Jerusalem artichokes tend to be ignored because of their uneven shape, which makes cleaning and peeling tiresome. It is possible to cook them in their skins and peel them afterwards, which is the best method when serving them as a vegetable. Jerusalem artichokes should be as firm as possible; if they feel spongy, do not buy them. Fresh, firm Jerusalem artichokes will store in the refrigerator for up to 2 weeks.

450 g (1 lb) Jerusalem artichokes
10 ml (2 tsp) lemon juice or vinegar
100 g (4 oz) onion, skinned
100 g (4 oz) carrot, peeled
2 sticks celery, washed
1.1 litres (2 pints) home made chicken stock or make up using 1 chicken stock cube
1 bay leaf

2.5 ml ($\frac{1}{2}$ level tsp) salt
6–8 twists of pepper from a mill or good pinch powder
1.25 ml ($\frac{1}{4}$ level tsp) nutmeg
chopped fresh parsley to garnish

Peel and slice the Jerusalem artichokes into a bowl of cold water to which you have added lemon juice or vinegar. Chop the onion, carrot and celery. Pour the stock into a medium sized saucepan and bring rapidly to the boil. Add the drained artichokes, all the vegetables and the bay leaf. Season with salt, pepper and nutmeg. Reduce the heat to low, cover and simmer for 30 minutes.

Cool slightly. Remove the bay leaf. Purée in a blender or use a mouli-legumes to purée the vegetables. Alternatively mash with a fork. Reheat gently and adjust the seasoning. Serve with a sprinkling of finely chopped parsley.

The soup may be thinned down with a little skimmed milk. Use single cream for a special occasion. This soup freezes well.

Serves 6

30 calories per serving
plus 15 ml (1 tbsp) single cream – 30 calories

'Leanline' onion soup

I usually make a large quantity of this soup as it requires a fair amount of preparation. However, quantities may be halved if preferred. I do find an electric slicer or the mouli-julienne slicing disc extremely useful for the tear-making task of thinly slicing all those onions.

1.7 litres (3 pints) home made chicken stock or make up using 2 chicken stock cubes

900 g (2 lb) onions, skinned (preferably Spanish)

100 g (4 oz) carrots, peeled

15 g ($\frac{1}{2}$ oz) butter

5 ml (1 level tsp) salt

10–12 twists of pepper from a mill or 1.25 ml ($\frac{1}{4}$ level tsp) powder

1.25 ml ($\frac{1}{4}$ level tsp) sugar

15 g ($\frac{1}{2}$ oz) wholemeal flour

5 ml (1 tsp) soy sauce

You will need to use a large saucepan of approximately 4–4.5-litres (7–8-pint) capacity. Prepare the stock in advance as it must be boiling when added to the cooked vegetables. Thinly slice the onions. Finely grate the carrots. Melt the butter over a low heat. Add the onions and carrots. Stir and turn them over. Cover the pan and cook slowly for 20 minutes, stirring the vegetables occasionally. Uncover and sprinkle in the salt, pepper and sugar, stirring well.

Increase the heat slightly and continue to cook, uncovered, for 20 minutes. Shake the pan and stir the vegetables from time to time to prevent burning. The onions will become tender, shiny and faintly coloured. Reduce the heat and stir in the flour. Cook for 2 minutes. Gradually stir in the boiling stock, with the soy sauce added, to prevent lumps from forming. Partially cover with a lid and simmer for 30 minutes. Check the seasoning and serve with Parmesan cheese and cubes of toasted wholemeal bread.

Note This soup freezes well.

Serves 8

---

55 calories per serving

plus 5 ml (1 level tsp) grated Parmesan cheese – 30 calories

25 g (1 oz) cubes toasted wholemeal bread – 60 calories

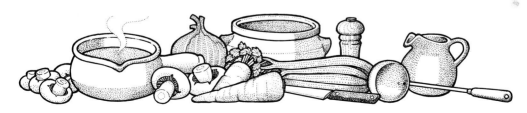

Celery and carrot soup

225–275 g (8–10 oz) celery, after
   trimming
15 ml (1 tbsp) chopped celery leaves
100 g (4 oz) carrot, peeled
50 g (2 oz) flat mushrooms
2 spring onions

1.4 litres (2½ pints) home made
   chicken stock or make up using
   2 chicken stock cubes with 5 ml
   (1 level tsp) tomato paste
5 ml (1 tsp) soy sauce
salt and freshly ground pepper

Trim the celery. Separate the stalks and wash thoroughly to remove all grit. Dry on kitchen paper. Shred the stalks crossways into very thin strips, about 0.3 cm (⅛ in). Cut the carrot into small cubes. Wash the mushrooms quickly in cold water. Rub them between the fingers to remove all dirt. Drain and pat dry on kitchen paper. Slice the mushrooms finely. Trim and clean the spring onions. Chop them finely.

Heat the stock to simmering point and add the soy sauce. Depending on its flavour, add a little salt and pepper. Tip the celery, carrots and spring onions into the boiling stock. Partially cover the pan and simmer for 10 minutes. The vegetables should be firm and crunchy. Stir in the sliced mushrooms. Cook them for a few minutes – just long enough to heat through.

Serves 6

25 calories per serving

Leek and carrot soup

Illustrated in colour facing page 28

450 g (1 lb) leeks
350 g (12 oz) carrots, peeled
900 ml (1½ pints) water
5 ml (1 level tsp) salt
1 bay leaf

6–8 twists of pepper from a mill or
   good pinch powder
150 ml (¼ pint) skimmed milk
single cream and chopped fresh
   parsley to garnish

The leeks we buy today are getting cleaner all the time and all but the coarse green end is usable. Trim and wash thoroughly in plenty of cold water. Slice thinly and soak for 10 minutes in lightly salted cold water. Drain and rinse in a colander to eliminate any last particles of grit. Grate the carrots using the mouli-julienne (disc no. 3) or a coarse grater. Measure the water into a saucepan, bring to the boil and add the salt and bay leaf. Add all the vegetables and bring back to the boil. Reduce to a low heat, add the pepper and simmer for 30 minutes. Soup should never boil rapidly; if necessary, partially cover with the lid to maintain gentle cooking.

Cool the soup slightly. Remove the bay leaf; purée in a blender or mouli-legumes, or mash the vegetables. Stir in the skimmed milk and adjust the seasoning before serving.

The soup may require thinning with water or skimmed milk – don't forget to count the calories. A little single cream and chopped parsley stirred into individual bowls looks very attractive. Shreds of carrot add a different texture and colour.

This soup will keep, covered, in the refrigerator for 4 days. It also freezes particularly well.
Serves 6

35 calories per serving
plus 15 ml (1 tbsp) single cream – 30 calories

Winter vegetable soup

225 g (8 oz) parsnips, peeled
100 g (4 oz) turnip, peeled
100 g (4 oz) carrot, peeled
100 g (4 oz) onion, skinned
15 g ($\frac{1}{2}$ oz) butter
2.5 ml ($\frac{1}{2}$ level tsp) mild curry powder

1.1 litres (2 pints) hot chicken stock
    made up using 1 chicken stock cube
5 ml (1 level tsp) salt
little freshly ground pepper
chopped chives to garnish (optional)

Coarsely grate or finely chop all the vegetables. Melt the butter over a low heat and add the vegetables. Stir until coated with the butter, cover and sweat the vegetables for 5 minutes. Sprinkle in the curry powder, stirring well into the vegetables. Allow to cook for 1 minute then pour in the hot stock and add the salt. Bring to the boil, cover and simmer for 30 minutes.

Cool slightly, then purée in a blender or press through a sieve to obtain a smooth creamy texture. Reheat gently, adjust the seasoning, adding just a little pepper, and if necessary thin down with a little stock. Just before serving, garnish with a sprinkling of chopped chives and tiny cubes of wholemeal bread baked in the oven without fat.
Serves 6

50 calories per serving
plus 25 g (1 oz) wholemeal bread – 60 calories

Lean watercress soup

1 100-g (4-oz) bunch watercress
225 g (8 oz) onion, skinned
225 g (8 oz) carrots, peeled
1.1 litres (1$\frac{1}{2}$ pints) home made
    chicken stock or make up using
    1 chicken stock cube

5 ml (1 tsp) lemon juice
2.5 ml ($\frac{1}{2}$ level tsp) salt
6–8 twists of pepper from a mill or
    good pinch powder
pinch nutmeg
watercress to garnish

Wash the watercress in plenty of cold, lightly salted water, snipping off any wilted leaves and trimming the coarsest stalks. Drain into a colander then chop the leaves and stalks together. These are cooked for the last 10 minutes only.

Finely chop the onion and carrots or coarsely grate them. Bring the stock to the boil in a medium saucepan and add the lemon juice, salt and pepper, onions and carrots. Reduce the heat to low, partially cover the pan and simmer gently for 15 minutes. Add the watercress leaves and stalks and continue cooking for 10 minutes.

Remove from the heat and allow to cool slightly. Purée in a blender or food mill. An alternative way is to sieve the onion and carrot mixture and finely chop the watercress. Just before serving, reheat gently and adjust seasoning, adding a little grated nutmeg. Garnish with chopped watercress. 5 ml (1 tsp) natural yogurt or 15 ml (1 tbsp) single cream may be stirred into each bowl. Store, covered, in a refrigerator for 3 days.
Serves 4

35 calories per serving
plus 5 ml (1 tsp) yogurt – 5 calories
15 ml (1 tbsp) single cream – 30 calories

Swede and cabbage soup

225 g (8 oz) swedes, peeled
225 g (8 oz) carrots, peeled
100 g (4 oz) onion, skinned
100 g (4 oz) white cabbage
15 g ($\frac{1}{2}$ oz) butter
1.1 litres (2 pints) hot chicken stock made up using 1 chicken stock cube

5 ml (1 level tsp) salt
freshly ground pepper or good pinch powder
150 ml ($\frac{1}{4}$ pint) skimmed milk
finely chopped fresh parsley to garnish

Coarsely grate the swedes, carrots and onion. Thinly slice or finely shred the cabbage using a mouli-julienne (disc no. 4) if possible. Melt the butter over a low heat and add all the vegetables. Stir until coated with the butter, cover the pan and sweat the vegetables for 5 minutes over a low heat. Turn and stir the glistening vegetables, then cover again and cook for a further 5 minutes. Pour in the hot stock, season with salt and pepper and bring to the boil. Cover or partially cover and simmer gently for 30 minutes.

Cool slightly. Purée all but a cupful of the vegetables in a blender or food mill, or press through a sieve. Mix together and stir in the skimmed milk. Reheat gently. Check the seasoning as pepper fades during cooking. Garnish with finely chopped parsley and swirl 15 ml (1 tbsp) single cream on each bowl of soup for a special occasion.
Serves 8

40 calories per serving
70 calories per serving (with single cream)

Turnip-turmeric soup

Although this delicious soup can be made using old turnips, try the early crop small variety as soon as they are available as they are full of flavour.

450 g (1 lb) turnips, peeled
100 g (4 oz) carrot, peeled
100 g (4 oz) onion, skinned
15 g (½ oz) butter
5 ml (1 level tsp) ground turmeric
5 ml (1 level tsp) salt

6–8 twists of pepper from a mill or good pinch powder
1.1 litres (2 pints) hot home made chicken or beef stock or make up using 1 chicken or beef stock cube
chopped fresh parsley to garnish

Thinly slice the turnips, carrot and onion. Melt the butter over a low heat and add the vegetables. Stir until coated with the butter, cover and sweat the vegetables for 15 minutes. Shake the pan about half way through and gently turn the vegetables, keeping the heat low so that they absorb the butter without burning. Sprinkle in the turmeric, stir and cook for 1 minute. Season with salt and pepper and pour in the hot stock. Cover and simmer for 30 minutes. Make sure the soup is simmering gently – tilt the lid of the pan if necessary.

Cool slightly, purée in a blender or mouli-legumes, or press through a sieve. Return the soup to the heat. It may be thinned down with 150 ml (¼ pint) skimmed milk or stock. Sprinkle with plenty of finely chopped parsley.
Serves 6

45 calories per serving
55 calories per serving (with skimmed milk)

Mustardy mushroom soup

275 g (10 oz) mushrooms
100 g (4 oz) onion, skinned
100 g (4 oz) carrot, peeled
15 g (½ oz) butter
900 ml (1½ pints) hot home made chicken stock or make up using 1 chicken stock cube
2.5 ml (½ level tsp) salt

little freshly ground pepper
1.25 ml (¼ level tsp) nutmeg
1 bay leaf
10 ml (2 level tsp) smooth mild French mustard
10 ml (2 tsp) lemon juice
30 ml (2 tbsp) single cream or 150 ml (¼ pint) skimmed milk

Wash the mushrooms quickly in a bowl of cold water, rubbing gently with the fingers to remove dirt. Drain and dry on kitchen paper. Leave aside 50 g (2 oz) mushrooms for finishing the soup. Slice or chop the rest including the stalks. Thinly slice the onion and carrot. Melt the butter over a low heat. Add the onion and carrot, stir and turn them over so that they glisten. Cover the pan and sweat them for 5 minutes.

Tip in the mushrooms. Stir again, cover and cook, still over very low heat, for a further 5 minutes. Pour in the hot stock, salt, pepper, nutmeg, bay leaf, mustard and lemon juice. Bring to the boil, cover and simmer for 30 minutes.

Cool the soup slightly, remove the bay leaf and purée in a blender or mouli-legumes, or press through a sieve. Just before reheating, add the 50 g (2 oz) reserved raw chopped mushrooms. When the soup is piping hot, stir in the cream or skimmed milk and pour into individual bowls.

Serves 6

---

50 calories per serving (with cream)
45 calories per serving (with skimmed milk)

Lean and easy tomato soup

This is a particularly useful soup as it contains no fat, is very low in calories and provides an ideal hot snack. Children adore it and adults usually ask for second helpings! Quantities may be doubled using a large can of tomatoes; for half quantity use the same size 397-g (14-oz) can tomatoes, and halve all the other ingredients.

100 g (4 oz) onion, skinned
225 g (8 oz) carrots, peeled
2 sticks celery with leaves, washed
1 clove garlic, skinned
397-g (14-oz) can Italian tomatoes
10 ml (2 tsp) tomato paste
1 bay leaf
1.25 ml ($\frac{1}{4}$ level tsp) dried marjoram

5 ml (1 tsp) salt
1.25 ml ($\frac{1}{4}$ level tsp) freshly ground black pepper
900 ml ($1\frac{1}{2}$ pints) hot chicken stock made up using 1 chicken stock cube
30 ml (6 tsp) natural yogurt and chopped fresh parsley to garnish

Slice or coarsely chop the vegetables, including the celery leaves and garlic. Tip into a saucepan together with the canned tomatoes and juice, tomato paste, bay leaf, marjoram, salt, freshly ground pepper and the hot stock. Bring to the boil, cover and simmer gently for 40 minutes.

Cool, remove the bay leaf and purée in a blender or press through a sieve. Reheat, pour into individual bowls and swirl 5 ml (1 tsp) natural yogurt over the surface. A teaspoon of finely chopped fresh parsley sprinkled onto each bowl is equally pleasing.

Serves 6

---

40 calories per serving

Leek and carrot soup (page 24) ▶

Starters

'Leanline' kipper pâté (page 32), Rosy curd cheese starter
(page 31), Wholemeal rolls (page 114)

With the appetite at its keenest, the first course is generally the most hazardous hurdle for weight-conscious diners. Therefore it must be satisfying, yet light and low in calories. Fish makes an ideal first course, hot or cold, its delicate flavours blending well with a variety of seasonings and other ingredients. Herby cheese mixtures are attractive; serve them with crisp salads or use as a stuffing.

Many of the recipes will enliven any cold buffet.

Herby cheese starter

There are countless calorie-laden cream cheeses available which tend to be expensive and cloyingly rich.

Low or medium fat curd cheese is an excellent alternative. This version uses it as a base for a starter incorporating a generous mixture of fresh herbs.

225 g (8 oz) curd cheese
15 ml (1 tbsp) natural yogurt
15 ml (1 tbsp) finely chopped parsley
30 ml (2 tbsp) finely chopped chives
1 small clove garlic, skinned
30 ml (2 tbsp) finely chopped
    watercress leaves

6–8 twists of pepper from a mill or
    good pinch powder
1.25 ml ($\frac{1}{4}$ level tsp) salt
1 lettuce, washed
watercress sprigs to garnish

Beat the cheese and yogurt together until smooth. Mix the herbs together. Chop the garlic very finely. Wash and dry the watercress, snipping away most of the stalks but leaving a few of the finer stalks for garnish. Chop the stalks and leaves. Work all these ingredients into the cheese and yogurt mixture. Season with pepper and salt.

Serve piled on to lettuce leaves. Surround with watercress sprigs. Excellent as a spread or stuffing (see Rosy curd cheese starter opposite). Stored, covered, in a refrigerator, this keeps for 3 days.

Serves 4

70 calories per serving

Rosy curd cheese starter

Illustrated in colour facing page 29

225 g (8 oz) curd cheese
15 ml (1 tbsp) natural yogurt
50 g (2 oz) tomato, skinned
1 medium red pepper
1 small onion, skinned
50 g (2 oz) ham, cut into thin strips or
    50 g (2 oz) prawns, chopped

2.5 ml ($\frac{1}{2}$ level tsp) sweet paprika
  pepper
3 drops Tabasco pepper sauce
freshly ground black pepper and salt

Beat the cheese and yogurt together until smooth. Remove the core and seeds from the tomato and chop the flesh. Deseed the red pepper and chop finely with the onion. Work all these ingredients, plus the ham or prawns, into the cheese and yogurt mixture.

Stir in the paprika pepper and Tabasco sauce. Season with a few twists of pepper from a mill and salt. The flavour should not be too hot. Add a little more paprika if necessary to strengthen the colour. This pale rosy cheese mixture makes a delightful dinner party starter. Use it as a stuffing for tomato halves, cucumber cups or celery. This starter may be stored, covered, in the refrigerator for 3 days.
Serves 6

70 calories per serving

Marinated kipper fillets

227-g (8-oz) packet kipper fillets
2 small onions, skinned
2 bay leaves
10 ml (2 tsp) oil (olive oil for the best
    flavour)
30 ml (2 tbsp) wine or cider vinegar

several twists of pepper from a mill
  or pinch powder
good pinch nutmeg, freshly grated if
  possible

Gently ease away the kipper skin. Place the fillets in a single layer in a shallow dish. Slice the onion into rings, crumble the bay leaves and spread them over the fillets.

Mix together the oil, vinegar, pepper and nutmeg. Pour the marinade over the fillets. Cover with foil and leave for several hours or overnight. Turn two or three times during the marinating period. This starter can also be served as a light supper dish and is attractive for open crispbread sandwiches, using a little cottage cheese and watercress leaves as a base.
Serves 4

100 calories per serving

'Leanline' kipper pâté

Illustrated in colour facing page 29

350 g (12 oz) whole kippers or fillets
    yielding 225–275 g (8–10 oz) flesh
    after boning and skinning
113-g (4-oz) carton cottage cheese
½ clove garlic, skinned

freshly ground pepper
1.25 ml (¼ level tsp) nutmeg
15 ml (1 tbsp) natural yogurt
juice of ½ small lemon
lemon and cucumber twists to garnish

Pour boiling water over the kippers to soften and remove excess salt. Leave for a minute then drain and dry on kitchen paper. Peel away the skin and remove bones.

Add the ingredients gradually to the blender, using the lemon juice and yogurt to produce a smooth pâté (see method opposite). A coarser pâté is obtained by working the ingredients together with a fork. Although some people object to the white flecks of cottage cheese, I find their presence infinitely preferable to the interminable task of pushing them through a sieve!

Garnish with lemon and cucumber twists and/or parsley sprigs. May be stored in the refrigerator for up to 5 days, double wrapped in foil to protect other foods from the smell. This pâté freezes well.

Serves 6

125 calories per serving

Smoked mackerel pâté

275 g (10 oz) smoked mackerel fillets
113-g (4-oz) carton cottage cheese
15–30 ml (1–2 tbsp) natural yogurt
finely grated rind and juice of ½
    lemon

10 ml (2 level tsp) raw grated
    horseradish or 10 ml (2 level tsp)
    horseradish relish
6–8 twists of pepper from a mill or
    good pinch powder

Remove the skin and any bones from the mackerel. Batch feed the ingredients into a blender using the lemon juice and yogurt to produce a smooth pâté.

Alternatively, mix all the ingredients together with a fork. This results in a coarser pâté but the flavour is just as good. Specks of cottage cheese will remain unless you are prepared to press it through a sieve. Adjust the seasoning; you may like a little more horseradish and lemon. Store, covered, in the refrigerator for up to 3 days.

Serves 6

120 calories per serving

Tarragon flavoured smoked mackerel pâté

275 g (10 oz) smoked mackerel fillets
113-g (4-oz) carton cottage cheese
15 ml (1 tbsp) natural yogurt
10 ml (2 tsp) lemon juice
5 ml (1 level tsp) tarragon mustard
  (available from good grocers)

2.5 ml ($\frac{1}{2}$ level tsp) dried tarragon
8–10 twists of pepper from a mill or
  1.25 ml ($\frac{1}{4}$ level tsp) powder

Remove the skin from the fish by gently lifting and pulling away from the flesh. Small bones will come away at the same time. Break up the fillets. If using an electric blender, add the cottage cheese, yogurt, lemon juice, mustard and dried tarragon and liquidise these ingredients before adding the mackerel. Drop the mackerel pieces on to the whirling blades through the hole in the lid. You may still need to scrape down the sides to help loosen the mixture, but the liquid ingredients should eliminate the clogging of the blades.

Season with the pepper only as smoked mackerel contains sufficient salt. A coarser pâté is equally delicious; mix everything together thoroughly with a fork.
Serves 6

120 calories per serving

Smoked cod's roe mousse

60 ml (4 tbsp) cold water
15-g ($\frac{1}{2}$-oz) packet gelatine
225 g (8 oz) smoked cod's roe
113-g (4-oz) carton cottage cheese
juice of $\frac{1}{2}$ lemon
141-g (5-oz) carton natural yogurt
1 clove garlic, skinned

6 twists of pepper from a mill or good
  pinch powder
2 drops Tabasco pepper sauce
sprinkling of sweet paprika pepper
chopped hard-boiled egg and/or
  finely chopped parsley to garnish

Put the 60 ml (4 tbsp) cold water into a small saucepan, sprinkle over the gelatine and leave to soak for a few minutes. Place over a very low heat to dissolve, stirring all the time with a metal spoon. Do not boil. Melting gelatine takes about 3 minutes and results in a smooth slightly cloudy syrup. Set aside to cool.

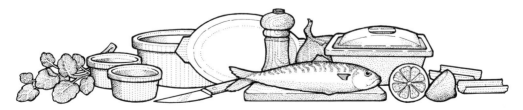

Using a metal spoon, scrape away the cod's roe from the skin. Place the roe in a blender goblet and purée together with the cottage cheese, lemon juice, yogurt and garlic, until the mixture is smooth and shiny. Stir in the pepper and Tabasco sauce. If no blender is available, use a fork to work all the ingredients together. The cottage cheese will remain lumpy unless it is pressed through a sieve.

To blend the cool gelatine into the mousse, switch the blender to low speed and pour the gelatine through the lid into the goblet. This takes about 3 seconds. Pour the mousse into a 600-ml (1-pint) soufflé dish. Cover and chill until set. This may take 2–3 hours in a refrigerator or longer in a cool larder. Just before serving, scatter the chopped egg and a little parsley over the surface. Add a sprinkling of paprika pepper.

Serves 6

---

60 calories per serving
plus 1 hard-boiled egg – 80 calories

Smoked fish mousse

550 g (1¼ lb) smoked fish fillet
about 450 ml (¾ pint) cold water to
  cover
1 onion, skinned
1 carrot, peeled
1 stick celery with leaves, washed
1 bay leaf
6 whole black peppercorns
a strip of lemon peel
15 ml (1 tbsp) wine vinegar
freshly ground black pepper and salt

pinch nutmeg
300 ml (½ pint) fish stock (see
  method)
15-g (½-oz) packet gelatine
5 ml (1 level tsp) dried tarragon
5 ml (1 level tsp) capers
15 ml (1 tbsp) chopped celery leaves
juice of ½ lemon
141-g (5-oz) carton natural yogurt
finely chopped parsley and crumbled
  hard-boiled egg yolk to garnish

Cut the fish into three or four pieces and put them in a wide shallow saucepan. Pour in sufficient cold water to cover. Add the thinly sliced onion, carrot, celery, bay leaf, peppercorns, lemon peel and vinegar. Cover the pan and bring slowly to the boil. Keep the heat as low as possible and cook the fish at a lazy simmer for 5–10 minutes until tender. Lift out the fish with a perforated spoon. Peel off the skin, remove any bones and roughly flake the flesh. Place in a large mixing bowl and season well with freshly ground pepper and nutmeg. Check for salt as the fish itself may be salty.

Boil the fish liquid rapidly, uncovered, for 5–10 minutes to reduce and concentrate the flavour. Strain 300 ml (½ pint) fish stock into a measuring jug. Put the gelatine in a small saucepan, stir in 150 ml (¼ pint) of the measured stock and dissolve over a gentle heat, stirring all the time. Do not boil. Mix this into the remaining fish stock and allow to cool.

When the flaked fish has cooled, stir in the dried tarragon, capers, finely chopped celery leaves and lemon juice. Then mix in the cold fish stock and check the seasoning before stirring in the yogurt. It is most important to season well to achieve a good flavour. Spoon into small ramekins or a medium sized soufflé dish. Loosely cover with foil and chill until set.

Remove from the refrigerator at least an hour before serving to allow the flavours to mellow. Garnish with crumbled hard-boiled egg yolk and finely chopped parsley.
Serves 6

110 calories per serving

Tuna and watercress starter

198-g (7-oz) can tuna
½ bunch watercress
50 g (2 oz) cottage cheese
15 ml (1 tbsp) natural yogurt
10 ml (2 tsp) lemon juice
5 ml (1 level tsp) smooth strong
  French mustard

6 twists of pepper from a mill or
  pinch powder (see method)
watercress leaves and spring onions,
  finely chopped, to garnish

Drain the tuna to remove excess oil. Wash the watercress in cold lightly salted water. Discard any wilted leaves and cut away the coarse stalks. Drain and dry thoroughly on kitchen paper or in a tea towel. If using a blender, chop the watercress by dropping it on to the whirling blades. Switch off before adding the cottage cheese, yogurt, lemon juice and mustard, and blend for a few seconds before adding the tuna. If you leave the heaviest ingredient until last, blending to a smooth texture takes seconds and you will not get clogged blades. Alternatively, work all the ingredients together with a fork.

Check the seasoning – if the mustard is sufficiently strong to season the pâté, pepper will not be necessary. Likewise, canned tuna tends to be sufficiently salty, for my taste anyway. Turn the pâté into a small soufflé dish or individual ramekins. Garnish with the watercress leaves and finely chopped spring onions.
Serves 4

95 calories per serving

Cold smoked fish with watercress dressing

This delicate tasting dish makes an excellent starter or main course. Serve it with a mixed green salad and quarters of hard-boiled egg.

450 g (1 lb) smoked haddock fillet
1 small onion, skinned
1 bay leaf
1 sprig of parsley and a few stalks
10 ml (2 tsp) lemon juice
a few twists of pepper from a mill or
    pinch powder
cold water to cover

5 ml (1 level tsp) mild grainy
    French mustard
5 ml (1 tsp) lemon juice
a few twists of pepper from a mill or
    pinch powder
a little salt
watercress sprigs to garnish

For the watercress dressing
½ bunch watercress
141-g (5-oz) carton natural yogurt

Cut the fish into four pieces. Lay them in a shallow saucepan with the onion, bay leaf, parsley, lemon juice and pepper. Pour in sufficient cold water to cover the fish. Cover the pan, bring slowly to the boil and simmer for 8–10 minutes, until the fish is tender but not falling to pieces. Remove the fish with a slotted spoon, peel away the skin and flake into a bowl.

Stir in the watercress dressing and pile on to a serving dish or into small ramekins. Garnish with sprigs of watercress.

For the dressing, wash the watercress in plenty of cold, lightly salted water. Drain and dry on kitchen paper. Cut away coarse stalks. Chop finely sufficient watercress to give 45 ml (3 tbsp). Tip the yogurt into a small bowl and stir in all the ingredients. Season lightly.

For a greener dressing use a blender to purée the watercress, lemon juice and 10 ml (2 tsp) yogurt then hand mix with the other ingredients. Blending all the ingredients will produce too liquid a dressing.
Serves 6

85 calories per serving

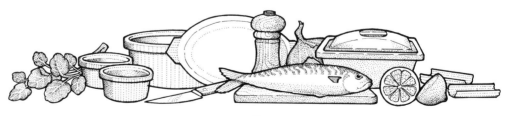

Stuffed tomatoes

6 medium firm tomatoes
salt
4 anchovies
skimmed milk
227-g (8-oz) carton cottage cheese
5 ml (1 level tsp) chopped capers
2 spring onions

1 hard-boiled egg
8–10 twists of pepper from a mill or
   good pinch powder
3 drops Tabasco pepper sauce
1.25 ml ($\frac{1}{4}$ level tsp) salt
50 g (2 oz) prawns, chopped
15 ml (1 tbsp) finely chopped parsley

Choose really firm tomatoes. Slice off the tops and scoop out the seeds using a grapefruit or serrated edged knife. Scrape away any residual seeds with a teaspoon. (Use the tomato pulp in soups or sauces.) Sprinkle the insides with salt and leave to drain upside down for 30 minutes. Soak the anchovies in a little skimmed milk for 30 minutes to remove excess salt. Drain, rinse in cold water and pat dry on kitchen paper.

Tip the cottage cheese into a medium size bowl. Chop the anchovies, capers, spring onions and egg. Mix into the cheese. Stir in the pepper, Tabasco sauce, salt, chopped prawns and parsley. Check the seasoning. Spoon the stuffing into the tomatoes and top with the lids. Serve with green salad.
Serves 6

80 calories per serving

Variation
Use 50 g (2 oz) canned crabmeat (40 calories) or 50 g (2 oz) lean ham (60 calories) instead of the prawns.

Avocado starter

2 medium ripe avocados, yielding
   225 g (8 oz) flesh
juice of $\frac{1}{2}$ lemon
50 g (2 oz) cottage cheese
2 spring onions or 1 button
   onion, finely chopped
$\frac{1}{2}$ clove garlic, crushed

3 drops Tabasco sauce
several twists of pepper from a
   mill or pinch powder
little salt
15 ml (1 tbsp) finely chopped
   fresh parsley

Halve the avocados and remove the stones. Scoop out the flesh with a spoon, sprinkle it with lemon juice and mash until smooth. Mix in all the other ingredients reserving a little parsley for garnish. Taste and adjust the seasoning. Spoon into individual ramekins.
Note This can be kept in the refrigerator, lightly covered with foil, for up to an hour. Avocado flesh discolours quickly but this can be delayed by sprinkling the surface of the prepared starter with a little lemon juice.

Variation
The cottage cheese may be replaced with curd cheese for a smoother mixture.
Serves 4

65 calories per serving

Fish

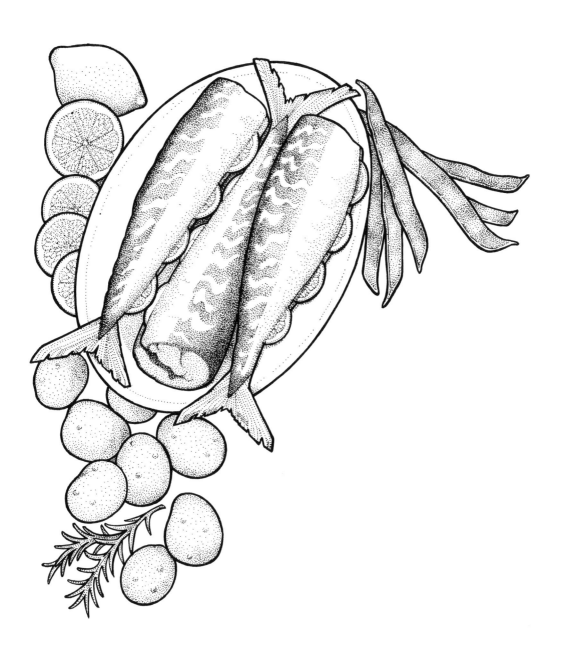

Fish, unfortunately, is still underused. Most fishmongers will fillet and clean it for you, so it is hard to understand why people remain resistant to the wide variety of reasonably priced fish available. As it is low in fat as well as calories it offers endless possibilities to the ambitious cook. On the other hand, choice fish, absolutely fresh, is always delightful when simply cooked.

It is worth cooking more than you need for one meal as cold leftovers make wonderful fish salads.

Hot smoked mackerel with spinach and mushrooms

250 ml (scant ½ pint) skimmed milk
  flavoured with
4 whole peppercorns
1.25 ml (¼ level tsp) freshly grated
  nutmeg (or powder)
1 bay leaf
a strip of lemon peel
½ clove garlic, skinned
1 small onion, skinned

225 g (8 oz) frozen spinach

pinch salt
6 twists of pepper from a mill or
  1.25 ml (¼ level tsp) powder
pinch nutmeg
350 g (12 oz) smoked mackerel fillets
15 g (½ oz) butter
100 g (4 oz) mushrooms, cleaned
2 spring onions, trimmed
15 g (½ oz) flour
5 ml (1 tsp) lemon juice
5 ml (1 tsp) smooth French mustard

Add the seasonings to the cold skimmed milk and leave for an hour to absorb the flavours.

The spinach should be completely thawed and drained of all water. Leave in a nylon sieve over a bowl and press gently with the back of a spoon to eliminate water. Season with the salt, pepper and nutmeg. Spread the drained and seasoned spinach over the bottom of a shallow ovenproof dish. Skin and roughly flake the mackerel and arrange it on the spinach.

Pour the milk and seasonings into a small heavy pan, place over low heat and bring very slowly to just below boiling point. Pour through a strainer into a measuring jug. Rinse and dry the pan and use it to make the sauce. Melt the butter over a low heat. Chop the mushrooms and spring onions finely and cook gently in the melted butter for 2–3 minutes. Sprinkle in the flour, stir well and cook for a few minutes to eliminate the raw taste. Gradually work in the hot seasoned milk, stirring all the time to obtain a smooth sauce. Increase the heat to moderate and bring the sauce to the boil, stirring continuously. Reduce the heat. Simmer for 2–3 minutes until the sauce has thickened slightly. Remove from heat and stir in the lemon juice, mustard and a little more seasoning to taste. Pour the

hot sauce over the fish. Reheat in the centre of the oven at 190°C (375°F) mark 5 for 15–20 minutes, depending on the depth of the dish.
Serves 4–6

200 calories per serving (for four – main course)
110 calories per serving (for six – starter)

Mushrooms and prawns in a light cheese sauce

225 g (8 oz) button mushrooms
50 g (2 oz) lean bacon
15 g ($\frac{1}{2}$ oz) butter
15 g ($\frac{1}{2}$ oz) flour
300 ml ($\frac{1}{2}$ pint) skimmed milk
5 ml (1 level tsp) grainy French
  mustard

6 twists of pepper from a mill or
  1.25 ml ($\frac{1}{4}$ level tsp) powder
1.25 ml ($\frac{1}{4}$ level tsp) nutmeg
a little salt according to taste
50 g (2 oz) Emmenthal or strong
  Cheddar cheese, grated
100 g (4 oz) prawns

Wash the mushrooms quickly in cold water. Drain and dry thoroughly on kitchen paper. Remove the mushroom stalks and chop finely. Trim off all the bacon fat. Scissor-snip the bacon into strips.

Melt the butter over a low heat, in a medium sized heavy saucepan. Raise the heat slightly, add the bacon and mushroom stalks and cook for a few minutes. Reduce the heat, stir in the flour and cook for another few minutes. Gradually work in the milk. Bring to the boil over moderate heat, stirring all the time. Lower the heat and stir in the mustard, seasonings and the mushrooms. Simmer slowly for another minute and stir in half the grated cheese. Add the prawns and lastly check the seasoning. Spoon into small ramekins or an ovenproof dish. Sprinkle with the remaining cheese. Reheat in the oven, one shelf above centre, at 190°C (375°F) mark 5 for 20–25 minutes, depending on the size and depth of the dish used. Delicious as a hot starter or light lunch or supper dish.
Serves 4 or 6

175 calories per serving (for four – main course)
115 calories per serving (for six – starter)

Fish balls

These fish balls are best made with fish stock but there is an alternative method which I give below. You will need the bones and skin of whichever fish you choose. Mackerel and white fish blend well.

700 g (1½ lb) mixed fish – 225 g (8 oz) mackerel and 450 g (1 lb) haddock or cod
100 g (4 oz) onion, skinned
100 g (4 oz) carrot, peeled
1 clove garlic, skinned
5 ml (1 level tsp) salt
8 twists of pepper from a mill or 1.25 ml (¼ level tsp) powder
1.25 ml (¼ level tsp) dried marjoram

pinch bay leaf powder
50 g (2 oz) breadcrumbs, at least one day old, preferably wholemeal
1 egg to bind
about 600 ml (1 pint) fish stock (see method)
1 bay leaf
a strip of lemon peel
sprig parsley

Have the mackerel skinned and filleted. Remove the skin and any bones from the white fish. (Keep all these trimmings if you don't have fish stock.) Mince the fish, onion, carrot and garlic together. Turn into a large mixing bowl. Add the salt, pepper, marjoram and bay leaf powder. Stir in the breadcrumbs and beaten egg. Roll into 5-cm (2-in) balls. Place the fish balls in a wide heavy-based saucepan, if possible in a single layer. Pour in the fish stock which should just cover them. If necessary add a little water with 15 ml (1 tbsp) of lemon juice or wine vinegar. Add the bay leaf, lemon peel and parsley. Partly cover with a lid, bring gently to the boil and simmer for 30 minutes.

If you do not have any fish stock, place the fish bones and skin in the saucepan. Carefully add the fish balls, bay leaf, a few parsley stalks, a thinly sliced onion and carrot. Season with 5 ml (1 level tsp) salt and 6 whole black peppercorns. Cover with cold water containing the juice of a lemon and a strip of peel. Cook as above, allowing 30 minutes from boiling point. Remove fish balls to a serving dish with a slotted spoon and strain stock over.

Serve hot with steamed new potatoes, carrots or a green vegetable.

Or serve cold as a starter, *or* with salad as a light main course.

Cool uncovered. These fish balls can be stored, covered, in the refrigerator for up to 2 days.

Note Alternatives to breadcrumbs are ground rice or semolina, both 100 calories per 25 g (1 oz). You may find a little less than 50 g (2 oz) sufficient. Breadcrumbs are 70 calories per 25 g (1 oz).

Serves 6

185 calories per serving

Smoked fish in a green sauce

This is an excellent supper dish. Serve with 'Leanline' baked potato halves (see page 86), lightly cooked courgettes and/or carrots.

450 g (1 lb) smoked haddock or cod fillet
5 ml (1 tsp) lemon juice
a strip of lemon rind (no pith)
1 small onion, skinned
1 bay leaf
a few parsley stalks
6 whole black peppercorns, lightly crushed
about 450 ml ($\frac{3}{4}$ pint) water to cover

For the sauce
15 g ($\frac{1}{2}$ oz) butter
15 g ($\frac{1}{2}$ oz) flour
150 ml ($\frac{1}{4}$ pint) hot fish stock (see method)
150 ml ($\frac{1}{4}$ pint) skimmed milk
freshly ground black pepper
good pinch nutmeg
30 ml (2 tbsp) finely chopped fresh parsley

Cut the fish into four pieces. Lay in a shallow saucepan with the lemon juice, rind, onion, bay leaf, parsley stalks and peppercorns. Pour in the cold water, bring slowly to the boil and simmer for 5–8 minutes until the fish is tender but not falling to pieces. (Unthawed frozen fish will need an extra 5 minutes.) Lift out fish pieces with a slotted spoon, peel away the skin and roughly flake. Spoon into an ovenproof dish. Measure 150 ml ($\frac{1}{4}$ pint) of the strained hot cooking liquid into a jug ready for the sauce.

To make the sauce, melt the butter over a low heat, sprinkle in the flour, stirring with a wooden spoon to obtain a smooth mixture and cook for 2 minutes. *Off the heat*, gradually work in the hot fish cooking liquid and then the skimmed milk. Return to a moderate heat and bring to the boil, stirring all the time. Reduce the heat to low and simmer for another 2 minutes. Remove and check the seasoning. Add a few twists of fresh pepper from a mill and a good pinch of nutmeg. Salt may not be necessary as the fish itself may have produced a salty stock. Stir in the chopped parsley. Pour the sauce over the fish. Reheat in the centre of the oven at 180°C (350°F) mark 4 for 25 minutes.

Serves 4

165 calories per serving

Plaice fillets in a wine and mushroom sauce

2 whole plaice
1 small onion, skinned
1 small carrot, peeled
1 bay leaf
a few parsley stalks
a strip of lemon peel
6 whole peppercorns
2.5 ml ($\frac{1}{2}$ level tsp) salt
150 ml ($\frac{1}{4}$ pint) dry white wine
150 ml ($\frac{1}{4}$ pint) water

For the sauce
100 g (4 oz) mushrooms
3 spring onions
15 g ($\frac{1}{2}$ oz) butter
15 g ($\frac{1}{2}$ oz) plain flour
30 ml (2 tbsp) single cream
freshly ground black pepper and salt
5 ml (1 tsp) lemon juice
15 ml (1 tbsp) finely chopped parsley

Divide the plaice into eight fillets. Sprinkle each fillet with a little seasoning. Thinly slice the onion and carrot and place them in a wide, shallow ovenproof dish. Add all the flavouring ingredients. Fold each fillet in three and arrange them over the vegetables in a single layer. Pour in the wine and water.

Cook, uncovered, in the centre of the oven at 180°C (350°F) mark 4 for 15 minutes.

Plaice fillets, folded in three, are cooked and served with a wine and mushroom sauce

44

Marinated baked tail end of cod (page 45), showing the fish before it has been cooked ▶

Remove the dish from the oven and lift out the fish. Strain the cooking liquid into a measuring jug. Replace the fish and keep warm in a very low oven. The liquid should measure 250 ml (under $\frac{1}{2}$ pint). If it is more than this, boil for 2–3 minutes until reduced.

Wash the mushrooms in a bowl of cold water. Dry thoroughly and slice thinly. Trim and clean the spring onions and chop finely. Melt the butter over a low heat in a small heavy saucepan. Add the mushrooms and spring onions and cook for 1 minute. Sprinkle in the flour, stirring well, and cook for another 1–2 minutes to eliminate the raw taste. Gradually work in the hot fish stock, stirring all the time to prevent lumps forming. Increase the heat slightly and bring the sauce to the boil, *stirring continuously*. Reduce the heat, stir in the cream and simmer for 2 minutes. Remove from the heat and season well with pepper, salt and lemon juice. Add the finely chopped parsley.

Pour the hot sauce over the fish fillets and reheat for 5 minutes in the centre of the oven at 190°C (375°F) mark 5.
Serves 4

180 calories per serving

Marinated baked tail end of cod

Illustrated in colour facing page 44

Buying whole fish is incredibly expensive, but tail end of cod makes an attractive alternative. This lightly spiced marinade produces moist, delicate flavoured fish. It is equally delicious hot or cold.

For the marinade	141-g (5-oz) carton natural yogurt
1 clove garlic, skinned	juice of 1 lemon
10 coriander seeds	30 ml (2 tbsp) finely chopped parsley
the seeds of 1 cardamom pod	
2.5 ml ($\frac{1}{2}$ level tsp) paprika pepper	1 medium onion, skinned
5 ml (1 level tsp) salt	1.1 kg ($2\frac{1}{2}$ lb) tail end of cod, trimmed
10 twists of pepper from a mill or	parsley stalks
1.25 ml ($\frac{1}{4}$ level tsp) powder	

Crush the garlic, spices and seasonings and stir them into the yogurt. Add the lemon juice and chopped parsley.

Thinly slice the onion and spread it over the base of a shallow ovenproof dish, large enough to contain the fish. Wipe the fish, trim if necessary and lay it on the onions. Put a few parsley stalks in the cavity. Pour the marinade over the fish, spooning a little inside. Leave in a cool place, not a refrigerator, for at least 1 hour, uncovered, or up to 6 hours if convenient and storage is sufficiently cool.

Baste the fish before covering the whole dish with foil. Cook in the centre of the oven at 190°C (375°F) mark 5 for 40 minutes. Remove from the oven, uncover and carefully peel

◀ *Braised leeks (page 82), Brown rice with beansprouts (page 94),*
'Leanline' dinner party beef casserole (page 60)

off the top skin. Spoon the marinade all over the surface. Return to the oven and cook, uncovered, for a further 25–30 minutes.

It is possible to serve the fish straight from the dish. Alternatively, lift it on to a heated serving dish and keep warm in the turned off oven – tip the sauce into a small saucepan, heat gently and pour over the fish. Serve hot or cold, with any leafy green vegetable, mushrooms or green beans.

Serves 6

130 calories per serving

Cod fillet in a piquant sauce

450 g (1 lb) cod fillet, skinned
a little pepper and salt
225 g (8 oz) leeks

For the marinade
141-g (5-oz) carton natural yogurt
juice of 1 lemon

10 coriander seeds, crushed
5 ml (1 level tsp) dried tarragon
1 bay leaf, broken into small pieces
2.5 ml ($\frac{1}{2}$ level tsp) salt
8 twists of pepper from a mill or good
    pinch powder

Choose thick pieces of fish and have the skin removed. Alternatively, it is quite easy to do it yourself: dry the fish and lay it on a board, dip a finger and thumb into salt and gently lift the skin, easing it away from the flesh. Cut the fish into 5 cm (2 in) wide pieces and sprinkle with a little pepper and salt. Place in a shallow dish.

To prepare the marinade, blend together the yogurt, lemon juice, crushed coriander seeds, herbs and seasonings in a small bowl. Coat the fish with the marinade and leave for 1 hour to absorb flavours. Trim the leeks and cut away the dark green stalk. Slice thinly and wash in plenty of cold water. Give them a short soak in lightly salted water if they are gritty. Drain and pat dry on kitchen paper. Place them in a wide heavy-based pan, cover and cook for 8–10 minutes over low heat. They will exude some of their own juices.

Carefully lay the fish pieces on the leeks and pour in the marinade. Cover the pan, increase the heat and rapidly bring to the boil. Cook briskly for 5 minutes. Reduce heat to very low and simmer for a further 10 minutes. With the point of a sharp knife test that the fish is tender. Do not overcook. Serve with spinach, fresh or frozen, or lightly boiled broccoli.

Serves 4

120 calories per serving
plus 100 g (4 oz) spinach – 30 calories
100 g (4 oz) broccoli – 15 calories

Baked mackerel with rosemary

Large mackerel, so often spurned by shoppers, make an economical family dish. Boned and baked in foil, it will even appeal to children. Large mackerel vary in size from 450–700 g (1–1½ lb) before boning.

700 g (1½ lb) mackerel (bought weight), boned	5 ml (1 level tsp) powdered rosemary
5 ml (1 level tsp) salt	1 clove garlic, skinned
6–8 twists of pepper from a mill or good pinch powder	a few thin lemon slices
	juice of ½ lemon

Clean and dry the fish. Sprinkle, inside and out, with salt, pepper and rosemary. Cut the garlic clove in half and place inside the fish. Lift the mackerel on to a sheet of foil, large enough to enclose the fish in a loose parcel. Lay the lemon slices inside and pour the lemon juice all over the fish. Make a loose tent-like parcel, folding the edges and twisting the ends of the package so that no juices escape.

Place on a baking sheet and cook in the centre of the oven at 190°C (375°F) mark 5 for 35 minutes. The cooked flesh will be tender and juicy. Serve with boiled new potatoes and boiled or steamed runner beans.

Serves 4

220 calories per serving
plus 100 g (4 oz) boiled new potatoes – 84 calories
100 g (4 oz) boiled or steamed runner beans – 8 calories

Baked fish parcels

This low calorie way of cooking fish is ideal for single diners, especially the housebound cook who may be starving by lunchtime. It is just as agreeable as an evening meal. A larger parcel, say up to four portions, may be used.

4 100-g (4-oz) fillets fresh haddock or cod or 4 frozen fish steaks	50 g (2 oz) green pepper
freshly ground pepper, salt and nutmeg (see method)	10 ml (2 tsp) grated raw onion or ½ onion squeezed on a lemon squeezer to obtain juice
225 g (8 oz) tomatoes	15 ml (1 tbsp) lemon juice, bottled or fresh
100 g (4 oz) mushrooms	

Lay each piece of fish in the centre of a square of foil, large enough to enclose the fish and other ingredients in a tent-like loose parcel. Season well with pepper, salt and nutmeg: it is difficult to give an exact quantity but fish does absorb a fair amount, so try 6 twists of pepper from a mill, a good pinch of salt and a shake of nutmeg on each piece of fish.

Skin the tomatoes by leaving in boiling water for 1 minute, or a fraction longer if the skin doesn't peel easily. Drain, skin and slice thickly. Wash the mushrooms in a bowl of cold water, rubbing between the fingers to remove dirt. Drain them and dry on kitchen paper. Thinly slice the mushrooms, including the stalks. Cut away the core and discard the seeds from the pepper. Wash in cold water, dry and cut into long thin strips. Top each fish portion with grated onion, followed by mushrooms, tomatoes and strips of pepper. Add a little more pepper and salt and sprinkle with the lemon juice.

Make a loose package with the foil, twisting the ends to make sure that the juices will be trapped inside the parcel. Place on a baking sheet. Bake in the centre of the oven at 190°C (375°F) mark 5 for 30 minutes. Allow an additional 10 minutes when cooked from frozen and test with the tip of a sharp knife before serving.

Try baking extra tomato halves and mushrooms at the same time, in a separate dish set on a shelf below the fish. Moisten with a little lemon juice and sprinkle with a little dried tarragon. Allow 15–20 minutes cooking time.
Serves 4

---

100 calories per parcel
plus calories for suggested accompaniments
50 g (2 oz) tomato – 10 calories
100 g (4 oz) mushrooms 8 calories
100 g (4 oz) jacket potato – 95 calories
15 g ($\frac{1}{2}$ oz) butter – 113 calories
15 g ($\frac{1}{2}$ oz) low fat spread – 55 calories

Baked fish in a rosy sauce

An excellent low calorie luncheon dish.

450 g (1 lb) whiting, cod or haddock
   fillets
pepper and salt
pinch nutmeg
50 g (2 oz) onion, chopped

For the sauce
100 g (4 oz) red pepper
141-g (5-oz) carton natural yogurt
10 ml (2 level tsp) tomato ketchup
5 ml (1 level tsp) tomato paste
2.5 ml ($\frac{1}{2}$ tsp) Worcestershire sauce

Cut the fillets into four pieces. Season with a little freshly ground pepper, salt and nutmeg. Spread the chopped onion over the base of a shallow ovenproof dish and lay the fish fillets on top.

Cut the red pepper in half, wash well, remove the core and seeds and dry on kitchen paper. Shred the flesh finely. In a small bowl, mix together the yogurt, tomato ketchup, paste and Worcestershire sauce. Stir in the shredded red pepper. Taste and add a very little pepper and salt if necessary. The ketchup and paste provide a certain amount of their own salt. Pour the sauce over the fish and bake in the centre of the oven at 200°C (400°F) mark 6 for 25–30 minutes, depending on the thickness of the fish. Allow 10 minutes extra if using frozen fish.

Note An alternative to red pepper is tomato flesh. Skin 2 tomatoes, cut them in half and gently scoop out the seeds. Dice the flesh and add this to the sauce.

Serves 4

115 calories per serving

Baked fish in a yogurt cheese sauce

450 g (1 lb) haddock or cod fillet
5 ml (1 level tsp) salt
6–8 twists of pepper from a mill or
  good pinch powder
1.25 ml ($\frac{1}{4}$ level tsp) nutmeg
5 ml (1 tsp) lemon juice

For the sauce

141-g (5-oz) carton natural yogurt
1 large egg yolk
good pinch dry mustard
15 g ($\frac{1}{2}$ oz) grated Parmesan or strong
  Cheddar cheese

Cut the fish into four pieces and lay them in a shallow ovenproof dish. Sprinkle with salt, pepper, nutmeg and lemon juice. In a small bowl, beat together the yogurt, egg yolk, mustard and cheese. Pour this over the fish.

Bake for 25 minutes near the top of the oven at 200°C (400°F) mark 6. Allow extra time if using frozen fish. Test with the tip of a pointed knife. The fish should be tender without flaking and the topping golden brown. Serve with 'Leanline' baked potato halves (see page 86) which can be cooked on the top shelf, baked tomato halves and mushrooms.

Serves 4

130 calories per serving

Lemon fish fillets

This is a useful and easy way to cook any flat fish. However, it is worth trying the cheaper fish, like dabs or Torbay sole, which I use regularly.

2 whole Torbay soles, divided into
  8 fillets
salt and pepper

100 g (4 oz) mushrooms
juice of $\frac{1}{2}$ lemon
15 g ($\frac{1}{2}$ oz) butter

Trim the fillets. Lay them flat on a board and sprinkle with a little salt and pepper. Roll them up, or fold in three if more convenient. Wash the mushrooms quickly in cold water and drain and dry on kitchen paper. Slice finely and spread them over the base of a shallow ovenproof dish. Lay the fillets on top. Pour the lemon juice over them. Add the butter, cut into 4 cubes. Cover the dish loosely with foil.

Bake in the centre of the oven at 190°C (375°F) mark 5 for 25 minutes. Remove the foil and cook for another 5 minutes. If using frozen fish, allow a little longer cooking time and cook uncovered.

Serves 4

---

130 calories per serving

Smoked fish and spinach pie

Smoked fish and spinach are perfectly matched ingredients. It is worth noting that frozen smoked fish together with frozen spinach produces a delicious standby meal.

227-g (8-oz) packet frozen spinach
salt, pepper and nutmeg
450 g (1 lb) filleted smoked haddock
   or cod
10 ml (2 tsp) lemon juice
strip of lemon peel
few parsley stalks
6 whole black peppercorns, lightly
   crushed
1 bay leaf
about 400 ml ($\frac{3}{4}$ pint) water

For the sauce
15 g ($\frac{1}{2}$ oz) butter
2.5 ml ($\frac{1}{2}$ level tsp) mild curry powder
15 g ($\frac{1}{2}$ oz) flour
300 ml ($\frac{1}{2}$ pint) hot fish stock
15 g ($\frac{1}{2}$ oz) Parmesan or strong
   Cheddar cheese, grated
several twists of pepper from a mill
1.25 ml ($\frac{1}{4}$ level tsp) grated nutmeg or
   powder

Prepare the spinach, which should be completely thawed and drained of all water. Leave in a nylon sieve over a pan and press gently with the back of a spoon to eliminate water. Sprinkle with a good pinch of salt, fresh pepper and nutmeg. Spread over the base of a 900-ml–1.1-litre ($1\frac{1}{2}$–2-pint) shallow ovenproof dish.

Cut the fish into four pieces. Place in a shallow saucepan together with the lemon juice, peel, parsley stalks, peppercorns and bay leaf and pour in just enough water to cover (don't drown the fish or you will have a weak and watery stock). Slowly bring to the boil and simmer for 5 minutes until the fish is tender but not falling to pieces. Frozen fish may need a few extra minutes. Remove from the heat, lift out the fish with a slotted spoon, peel away the skin and roughly flake. Strain 300 ml ($\frac{1}{2}$ pint) of the hot cooking liquid into a jug to make the sauce.

For the sauce, melt the butter over a low heat, sprinkle in the curry powder and flour and cook for 2 minutes, stirring all the time. Off the heat, gradually add the liquid in very small amounts, stirring to keep the sauce smooth. Return to a moderate heat and bring to the boil, stirring continuously. Reduce the heat and simmer for 2 minutes. Remove, taste and adjust seasoning. Salt may not be necessary as the smoked fish may itself produce a salty stock. Nutmeg is a delightful flavour for this dish.

Tip the flaked fish into the sauce and pour it over the spinach base. Sprinkle with the cheese and reheat in the centre of the oven at 190°C (375°F) mark 5 for 20 minutes. 'Leanline' baked potato halves (see page 86), so good with this dish, should be cooked in the hottest part of the oven, allowing 40–50 minutes cooking time. For a lower calorie count, try carrots simmered in water with a hint of lemon juice and a little salt until barely tender – about 5 minutes for new and 7 minutes for old.
Serves 4

180 calories per serving
plus 100 g (4 oz) carrots – 20 calories

Grilled trout with lemon and tarragon

Choose trout 225–275 g (8–10 oz) in weight.

For each trout
8 twists of pepper from a mill
  or good pinch powder
5 ml (1 level tsp) salt

5 ml (1 tsp) oil
few fresh or 5 ml (1 level tsp)
  dried tarragon leaves
juice of $\frac{1}{2}$ lemon

Have the trout gutted but leave on the head. Cut away the fins and part of the tail as these tend to burn easily, then rinse and dry the trout.

Sprinkle each fish inside and out with pepper and salt. Cut 3 diagonal slashes on both sides to allow heat to penetrate. Moisten with oil, place the fresh tarragon leaves inside the fish or sprinkle with dried tarragon. Spoon over the lemon juice. Preheat the grill to moderately hot. Place the trout about 15 cm (6 in) below the flame and grill for 5–8 minutes on each side, depending on the thickness of the fish. Finally, sprinkle with more lemon juice and finely chopped fresh or a little dried tarragon.

Serve with new potatoes and a green salad.
Note If possible, prepare fish an hour before grilling so that it fully absorbs the lemon and tarragon flavours.

300 calories per 275-g (10-oz) trout
100 g (4 oz) boiled new potatoes – 85 calories

Meat

These recipes demonstrate particularly clearly the principles underlying 'Leanline' techniques.

Visible fat has to be removed from the meat before cooking. Even so, it will be necessary to skim fat from the surface at the end of cooking. The easiest way, if time permits, is to allow the dish to cool completely. Drain the liquid into a bowl, cover and leave it in the refrigerator for several hours or overnight. Any fat will congeal on the surface in a solid layer, which is simple to lift off. However, there are times when it is more convenient to remove fat while the dish is hot. Allow it to cool slightly, so that the fat rises to the surface. Tilt the pan so that the fat accumulates at one side, and with a metal spoon, skim off as much fat as possible. In many instances the warm-skimming method will be sufficient, as a *little* residual fat gives body to robust sauces.

Meat is cooked in well-flavoured stock or wine and sealed in the aromatic steam trapped below the lid. Fat is kept to the absolute minimum, usually a teaspoon of oil. A heavy-based pan (see Equipment, page 12) is essential for success. Marinades are used to tenderise and season meat and poultry.

Roasting
Roasting without fat is totally successful, using instead yogurt, lemon and orange, herbs and spices to moisten and flavour the flesh. Gravy is made from natural juices together with a little stock or wine. Any residual fat is poured away and a little liquid is poured into the roasting pan and thoroughly worked into the highly flavoured drippings. It is tipped into a saucepan to reheat.

Thickening gravies and sauces
I rarely thicken gravy, but a practical method is to blend 10 ml (2 level tsp) cornflour with 15 ml (1 tbsp) cold water or stock, and stir this into the hot gravy. Simmer for 2–3 minutes until it slightly thickens.

Yogurt, blended with 10 ml (2 level tsp) cornflour, will enrich and thicken a sauce. Simply stir it into the casserole 5–10 minutes before serving.

Rich meat sauce

100 g (4 oz) carrots, peeled	30 ml (2 level tbsp) tomato paste
100 g (4 oz) onions, skinned	8–10 twists of pepper from a mill or
1 stick celery, washed	1.25 ml ($\frac{1}{4}$ level tsp) powder
10 ml (2 tsp) chopped celery leaves	2.5 ml ($\frac{1}{2}$ level tsp) salt
25 g (1 oz) lean bacon rashers	1.25 ml ($\frac{1}{4}$ level tsp) nutmeg
2 tomatoes, skinned	5 ml (1 level tsp) dried oregano or
5 ml (1 tsp) oil	marjoram
450 g (1 lb) lean minced beef	1 bay leaf
1 wine glass red wine	300 ml ($\frac{1}{2}$ pint) boiling water

The most practical type of pan for this sauce is a flameproof casserole. Otherwise, use a heavy-based saucepan. Transfer the sauce to an ovenproof container for slow oven simmering.

Finely chop the carrot, onion, celery and leaves. Scissor snip the bacon into tiny strips. Quarter the tomatoes. Heat the oil over low heat. Add the bacon and allow to cook for a few minutes. Stir in the chopped carrot, onion, celery and leaves. Cover the pan and cook for 5 minutes. Turn the vegetables over and over to coat them with the oil and juices. Crumble in the meat. Increase the heat to moderately hot, cover the pan and cook briskly for 5 minutes. The aromatic steam trapped beneath the lid will seal the meat. Continue cooking for a few more minutes if the meat is still slightly raw. Uncover, turn and stir the meat and vegetables until the meat is no longer showing any raw patches. Pour in the wine, boil for 1 minute and reduce to a very low heat.

Add the peeled and quartered tomatoes. Stir in the tomato paste, the seasonings and herbs. Gradually add most of the hot stock. The sauce should be thick and creamy. Add remaining stock if the sauce looks a little dry during cooking. Or add a little stock when reheating. Peel the clove of garlic, cut in half and crush it in 2.5 ml ($\frac{1}{2}$ level tsp) salt. Use a sharp knife and work it to a paste, then stir into the sauce until every speck has disappeared. This ensures that every trace is absorbed by the sauce and no one will be offended by the taste or smell. Cover the pan and cook over the lowest heat for at least 1 hour or transfer to the oven at 140°C (275°F) mark 1 for 1$\frac{1}{2}$–2 hours.

Before serving, check and adjust the seasoning. A little extra nutmeg and a pinch of dried herbs may be necessary after the lengthy simmering. If liked, serve with a sprinkling of Parmesan cheese. To store the sauce, allow to cool, uncovered. It will keep in the refrigerator, securely covered with a double layer of foil, for at least 3 days. It freezes well too.

To reheat, bring to boiling point over a medium heat, stirring all the time. Cover and cook gently for 30–40 minutes.

Serves 6

230 calories per serving
plus 7 g ($\frac{1}{4}$ oz) grated Parmesan cheese – 30 calories

Family meat sauce

100 g (4 oz) onions, skinned
100 g (4 oz) carrots, peeled
2 sticks celery with leaves, washed
5 ml (1 tsp) oil
450 g (1 lb) lean minced beef
396-g (14-oz) can Italian tomatoes
1 bay leaf
5 ml (1 level tsp) dried oregano or
  marjoram

2.5 ml (½ level tsp) salt
8–10 twists of pepper from a mill or
  1.25 ml (¼ level tsp) powder
good pinch nutmeg
15 ml (1 level tbsp) tomato paste
1 clove garlic, skinned
100 g (4 oz) mushrooms

Grate or finely chop the onions, carrots, celery and leaves. Gently heat the oil in a heavy-based saucepan. Add the vegetables, cover the pan and cook for 5 minutes. Stir and turn the vegetables. Crumble in the meat, increase the heat to medium, cover the pan and cook for another 5 minutes. Turn and stir the meat and vegetables until the meat is sealed and is no longer showing raw patches. Reduce the heat to low; add the tomatoes, bay leaf, herbs and seasoning. Work in the tomato paste.

Crush the garlic clove with a little salt and stir it into the sauce. Wash the mushrooms quickly in cold water removing the dirt with the fingertips. Drain and dry on kitchen paper, slice thinly and add to the sauce. Cover the pan and cook at a gentle simmer for 1 hour or transfer to the oven at 140°C (275°F) mark 1 and cook for 1 hour or longer, up to 2 hours. Check and adjust seasoning just before serving. If liked, serve this sauce with spaghetti.

To store, cool uncovered. It will keep in the refrigerator, covered with a double layer of foil, for at least 3 days. To reheat, bring to the boil over a medium heat, stirring all the time (add a couple of tablespoons of water if it looks a little dry). Reduce the heat, cover and simmer for 30–40 minutes until it is really hot.

Serves 6

---

190 calories per serving
plus 25 g (1 oz) raw spaghetti – 100 calories
50 g (2 oz) boiled spaghetti – 60 calories
(Boiled spaghetti loses a good deal of starch and absorbs a large amount of water.)

Beef braised in white wine

900 g (2 lb) lean stewing beef, cut in
  2 cm ($\frac{3}{4}$ inch) thick slices
225 g (8 oz) onions, skinned
100 g (4 oz) carrots, peeled
1 clove garlic, skinned
15 ml (1 tbsp) finely chopped celery
  leaves
2.5 ml ($\frac{1}{2}$ level tsp) dried marjoram
5 ml (1 level tsp) salt
2.5 ml ($\frac{1}{2}$ level tsp) freshly ground
  pepper or 1.25 ml ($\frac{1}{4}$ level tsp)
  powder
1 bay leaf, crumbled
2 cloves

150 ml ($\frac{1}{4}$ pint) dry white wine
25 ml (1 fl oz) gin (optional)
25 g (1 oz) lean bacon, fat removed
175 g (6 oz) mushrooms
397-g (14-oz) can Italian tomatoes,
  well-drained
15 g ($\frac{1}{2}$ oz) wholemeal flour

Wipe the beef and trim away all visible fat. Frozen meat should be slowly thawed, preferably in a refrigerator, and thoroughly dried before mixing with the marinade. Cut the beef into roughly 5-cm (2-in) pieces. Thinly slice the onions and carrots. Crush the garlic in a little salt.

Layer the beef, vegetables (including celery leaves), seasonings and herbs into a large deep bowl. Add the garlic, crumbled bay leaf and cloves. Measure the wine and gin, if used, into a jug and pour over the meat and vegetables. Cover and leave to marinate for 3–6 hours. Turn all the ingredients two or three times.

Snip the bacon into tiny strips. Wash the mushrooms quickly in cold water, drain and dry thoroughly on kitchen paper. Slice thinly. Drain the tomatoes in a nylon strainer, reserving the juice. Lift the pieces of beef from the marinade with a perforated spoon and place in a colander to drain away surplus moisture. Pat dry on kitchen paper and sprinkle with the flour.

Place the bacon, a layer of the marinade vegetables and half the tomatoes and mushrooms in a flameproof casserole. Spread the meat over the vegetables in a single layer. Add the rest of the vegetables and pour in the wine. Cover and place over a moderately fast heat. Bring to simmering point and bubble for 5 minutes, then reduce the heat. Stir in sufficient tomato juice to barely cover the contents.

Double cover the casserole, first with a sheet of foil, then with the lid. Simmer for 10 minutes before placing in the oven at 150°C (300°F) mark 2, one shelf below centre. Cook for 2 hours. Just before serving, skim off any fat. Adjust the seasoning.
Serves 6–8

300 calories per 100-g (4-oz) serving
400 calories per 175-g (6-oz) serving
plus 25 ml (1 fl oz) gin – 60 calories

Beef and leek pie

For the seasoning mixture
1 small onion
1 clove garlic, skinned
2.5 ml ($\frac{1}{2}$ level tsp) crushed coriander
    seeds
5 ml (1 level tsp) salt
2.5 ml ($\frac{1}{2}$ level tsp) freshly ground
    pepper or 1.25 ml ($\frac{1}{4}$ level tsp)
    powder

450 g (1 lb) lean minced beef
450 g (1 lb) leeks
salt
freshly ground pepper
pinch nutmeg
225 g (8 oz) tomatoes, skinned and
    sliced
50 g (2 oz) mushrooms, cleaned and
    sliced
2.5 ml ($\frac{1}{2}$ level tsp) dried oregano

Prepare the seasoned meat at least 1 hour in advance of cooking so that the flavour develops. It may be left, covered, in a refrigerator during the day and used in the evening.

The onion, garlic and coriander can be crushed in a blender. Alternatively, grate or finely chop the onion and crush all the other seasonings using a pestle and mortar, or a flat-bottomed small basin and the end of a rolling pin. Add the seasoning mixture to the meat and work to a fairly smooth texture.

To prepare the leeks, trim away the coarse dark green stalks and slice into thin rounds. Wash thoroughly in plenty of cold water. A short soak in cold water with 5 ml (1 level tsp) salt added often helps remove clinging grit.

Have ready a large saucepan of boiling water with 10 ml (2 level tsp) salt added. Cook the drained leeks for 7–10 minutes over medium heat, with the lid tilted, until tender. Drain well.

To assemble the pie, place the leeks in the bottom of a 1.1-litre (2-pint) ovenproof dish. Sprinkle with a little pepper and nutmeg and pour 30 ml (2 tbsp) cold water over them. Spread the seasoned meat over the leeks.

Cover with the tomatoes and mushroom slices. Season with a little pepper, salt and dried oregano. Cook in the centre of the oven at 190°C (375°F) mark 5 for 1 hour. Serve with 'Leanline' baked potato halves (see page 86) and a leafy green vegetable.

Serves 4–6

---

320 calories per serving (four)
215 calories per serving (six)

Very 'Leanline' beef casserole

This is a simple comforting dish, particularly low in calories and containing no added fat. It is worth making a large quantity as it reheats beautifully in a very slow oven. When freezing, do not include the garlic until the reheating stage, and remember, the cooked pieces of meat should not be in rags – a common fault with precooked frozen meat. Therefore give it less cooking time when it's for the freezer, say $1\frac{1}{2}$ hours, depending upon toughness of the meat. It really is necessary to check this during the cooking process.

900 g (2 lb) lean stewing beef – chuck, shin or shoulder
15 g ($\frac{1}{2}$ oz) wholemeal or plain flour
5 ml (1 level tsp) salt and 1.25 ml ($\frac{1}{4}$ level tsp) black pepper or good pinch powder
175 g (6 oz) onions, skinned
100 g (4 oz) carrots, peeled
1 clove garlic, skinned
5 ml (1 level tsp) coriander seeds, crushed

225 g (8 oz) tomatoes
5-cm (2-in) strip of orange rind, pith removed
150 ml ($\frac{1}{4}$ pint) stock made up using $\frac{1}{4}$ beef stock cube
5 ml (1 tsp) Worcestershire sauce
5 ml (1 level tsp) tomato paste

Trim away all visible fat and cut the meat into 4-cm ($1\frac{1}{2}$-in) chunks. Mix the flour with salt and pepper and sprinkle over the meat. Grate the onions and carrots. Crush the garlic and coriander seeds together. Peel and thickly slice tomatoes. (Just cover with boiling water for 1 minute and the skins will peel off easily.)

Layer the grated vegetables and meat in an ovenproof casserole. Bury the orange rind in the centre. Mix the stock with the Worcestershire sauce, tomato paste, crushed coriander seeds and garlic. Pour this into the casserole. Lay the sliced tomatoes over the surface. Cover the casserole first with a sheet of foil, then with the lid. Cook in the centre of the oven at 190°C (350°F) mark 4 for 1 hour.

Reduce the heat to 140°C (275°F) mark 1 for another hour. If the casserole is to be reheated, cook for $1\frac{1}{2}$ hours only. For reheating, place over moderate heat until the contents are really hot and bubbling, reduce to low and simmer for 30 minutes. Or bring up to boiling point and simmer in the oven. To store, always cool uncovered and refrigerate or freeze in a covered container.
Serves 8

250 calories per serving

'Leanline' dinner party beef casserole

Illustrated in colour facing page 45

900 g (2 lb) lean stewing beef – chuck
  steak or shin
15 g ($\frac{1}{2}$ oz) wholemeal flour
5 ml (1 level tsp) dried oregano
2.5 ml ($\frac{1}{2}$ level tsp) sweet paprika
  pepper
1.25 ml ($\frac{1}{4}$ level tsp) nutmeg
12 twists of pepper from a mill or 1.25
  ml ($\frac{1}{4}$ level tsp) powder
5 ml (1 level tsp) salt
225 g (8 oz) onions, skinned
225 g (8 oz) carrots, peeled

3 sticks celery with leaves
225 g (8 oz) turnips, peeled
1 clove garlic, skinned
225 g (8 oz) button mushrooms
300 ml ($\frac{1}{2}$ pint) home made stock or
  make up using $\frac{1}{2}$ stock cube
10 ml (2 level tsp) tomato paste
100 ml (4 fl oz) red wine
1 bay leaf
2 whole cloves
a sprig of parsley and a few extra
  stalks

Wipe the meat, trim away all visible fat and cut into 4 cm ($1\frac{1}{2}$-in) chunks. Mix the flour with the oregano, paprika, nutmeg, pepper and salt. Sprinkle over the meat. Grate the vegetables, using the mouli-julienne (disc no. 3) or the coarse side of a hand grater, or chop the onions, slice the carrots and celery and dice the turnips. Crush the garlic. Wash the mushrooms quickly in cold water. Drain and dry on kitchen paper. Do not add to the casserole at this stage. Bring the stock to the boil and stir in the tomato paste.

Use a flameproof casserole if possible. Otherwise use a heavy-based saucepan for the initial cooking, then layer all the ingredients into a suitable ovenproof casserole. Layer the vegetables and seasoned meat in a pan using half the vegetables for the first layer, then the meat and the rest of the vegetables. Pour in the wine, cover the pan, place over a brisk heat and cook for 5 minutes. During this time the wine bubbles, juices are released from the vegetables and steam is trapped under the lid, and this will seal the meat. Reduce the heat slightly. Add the boiling stock, replace the lid and cook again for a few minutes until the meat is no longer showing any raw patches. Reduce the heat to low. Add bay leaf, cloves, parsley and stalks, garlic and, if necessary, a little water – the meat should not be swimming in liquid.

Cover the pan with a sheet of foil, then put on the lid. Place one shelf below centre of the oven at 190°C (350°F) mark 4 for 30 minutes. Reduce the heat to 150°C (300°F) mark 2 for 1 hour. Check half way through cooking to see that a lazy simmer is maintained. Remove the casserole from the oven, add the mushrooms and simmer for a further 15 minutes. The total cooking time is about $1\frac{3}{4}$ hours. Adjust the seasoning.

If the casserole is to be reheated before serving, cook for $1\frac{1}{2}$ hours only. Cool uncovered.

Serves 8

280 calories per serving

Beef kebabs in a horseradish marinade

This quantity is sufficient for 4 skewers. Use long, flat-edged skewers and pack the contents close together. Keep the ends of the skewers clear so that you can turn them during cooking.

450 g (1 lb) (after trimming) tender beef – top rump or topside – cut in one thick slice
100 g (4 oz) green pepper
8 button onions

For the marinade
30 ml (2 level tbsp) natural yogurt

10 ml (2 level tsp) grated horseradish
5 ml (1 level tsp) dried marjoram
juice of 1 lemon, about 30 ml (2 tbsp)
6 twists of pepper from a mill or pinch powder
2.5 ml ($\frac{1}{2}$ level tsp) salt
2 bay leaves, broken into pieces

Trim the meat and cut into 2.5-cm (1-in) cubes. Halve the pepper; remove core and seeds. Wash in cold water, dry and cut into pieces slightly larger than the cubes of meat. Peel the onions and simmer them for 5 minutes in lightly salted boiling water. Drain thoroughly. Lay the meat and onions in a shallow dish, preferably in one layer.

Mix together all the marinade ingredients and spoon it over the meat. Leave in a cool place for 2–3 hours, turning once. Thread the meat, onions, pepper and broken bay leaves on to the skewers. Preheat the grill to high. Cook the kebabs for 10 minutes, not too close to the flame, basting with the marinade and turning two or three times. The meat should be a rich dark brown on the outside and slightly pink inside – really succulent. Serve with plain boiled rice and a green salad.
Serves 4

220 calories per serving
plus 50 g (2 oz) boiled rice – 70 calories

Variations
Mushrooms, tomato halves or sweet red peppers make attractive additions. Instead of beef, try cubes of lean pork, lamb or tiny meatballs. Meatballs require gentle grilling for

15–20 minutes. The marinade may be changed. Leave out the horseradish and add 15 ml (1 tbsp) grated raw onion and a crushed clove of garlic. Dried herbs add variety, but if they are available, fresh herbs, particularly thyme, are especially good for flavouring marinades.

Meat and spinach meatballs in tomato juice

Combining meat and vegetables is an effective way to stretch the budget and reduce the calories. Spinach blends particularly well with beef and tomato flavours. These colourful meatballs look most attractive on a bed of pale, crisply cooked cabbage. I use frozen spinach for blending as it is available all the year round, has a good flavour, and is certainly a time-saver.

227-g (8-oz) packet frozen spinach
salt and freshly ground pepper
pinch nutmeg
450 g (1 lb) lean minced beef – chuck
  or shin
2.5 ml (½ level tsp) cinnamon
1.25 ml (¼ level tsp) nutmeg
8–10 twists of pepper from a mill or
  good pinch powder
5 ml (1 level tsp) salt
2.5 ml (½ level tsp) dried marjoram or
  oregano

1 small onion, skinned and very finely
  chopped or grated

For the sauce
397-g (14-oz) can tomato juice
1 bay leaf
a few parsley stalks, if available

The spinach must be thoroughly drained of all its water. Thaw or cook if used straight from the freezer. Leave to drip in a nylon strainer, pressing out the water with the back of a spoon. Sprinkle with a little salt, nutmeg and pepper.

In a large bowl, mix together the meat and spinach, all the seasonings, marjoram and onion. Use an electric beater or wooden spoon, working everything together until you have a smooth pasty mixture. With wetted hands, roll into walnut-size balls – makes about 26–28 meatballs. Place them in two layers in a wide saucepan or casserole. Pour in the

tomato juice and add the bay leaf and parsley stalks. Cover and bring to the boil over a medium heat. Reduce to very low and simmer for 40 minutes. Serve with Lemony cabbage (see page 87).
Serves 4

315 calories per serving

Piquant lamb stew

150 ml ($\frac{1}{4}$ pint) boiling water
50 g (2 oz) unsweetened dessicated coconut
700 g ($1\frac{1}{2}$ lb) lean leg of lamb
15 g ($\frac{1}{2}$ oz) wholemeal flour mixed with 2.5 ml ($\frac{1}{2}$ level tsp) salt and 10 twists of pepper from a mill or good pinch powder
175 g (6 oz) onions, skinned
175 g (6 oz) carrots, peeled
1 stick celery with leaves, washed

1 175-g (6-oz) aubergine
5 ml (1 tsp) oil
5 ml (1 level tsp) curry powder
5 ml (1 level tsp) ground turmeric
300 ml ($\frac{1}{2}$ pint) home made chicken stock or make up using 1 chicken stock cube
10 ml (2 level tsp) tomato paste
10 ml (2 tsp) lemon juice
1 clove
10 ml (2 level tsp) mango chutney

Pour the 150 ml ($\frac{1}{4}$ pint) boiling water over the coconut to make coconut milk. Leave to infuse for 1 hour. Strain into a jug, pressing the coconut with the back of a spoon to extract the milk.

Trim away all visible fat from the lamb and cut into 2.5-cm (1-in) cubes. Sprinkle the seasoned flour over the meat. Grate or finely chop the onions and carrots. Chop the celery into small dice. Peel the aubergine and cut into small cubes.

Heat the oil in a heavy-based casserole or saucepan over a low heat. Stir in the grated vegetables, celery and leaves. Cover and cook gently for 5 minutes. Add the aubergine, mix into the vegetables and cook for a few minutes. Stir the curry powder and turmeric into the vegetables and cook for 2 minutes to eliminate the raw taste. Lay the floured meat on the bed of softened vegetables. Add the hot stock, coconut milk, tomato paste, lemon juice and clove. Stir in the chutney. Cover the pan and cook at a gentle simmer for $1\frac{1}{2}$ hours. Skim the fat from the surface and serve very hot. Serve with plain boiled rice and celery or runner beans to mop up the juices.
Serves 6

270 calories per serving
plus 50 g (2 oz) boiled rice—70 calories
100 g (4 oz) lightly cooked runner beans – 10 calories
100 g (4 oz) boiled celery – 10 calories

Aromatic lamb casserole

900 g (2 lb) lean boned leg of lamb
150 ml ($\frac{1}{4}$ pint) chicken stock made up
    using $\frac{1}{4}$ chicken stock cube
5 ml (1 level tsp) tomato paste

For the marinade
1 175-g (6-oz) onion, skinned
1 clove garlic, skinned

2.5 ml ($\frac{1}{2}$ level tsp) coriander seeds
2.5 ml ($\frac{1}{2}$ level tsp) ground ginger
10 twists of pepper from a mill or 1.25
    ml ($\frac{1}{4}$ level tsp) powder
5 ml (1 level tsp) salt
juice of 1 small lemon, about
    30 ml (2 tbsp)
141-g (5-oz) carton natural yogurt

Trim away all visible fat and cut the lamb into small chunks, about 4 cm ($1\frac{1}{2}$ in). All the marinade ingredients can be mixed together in an electric blender. Blend the liquid marinade ingredients and spices and then drop in pieces of onion and garlic through the lid on to the whirling blades. Alternatively, grate or finely chop the onion, crush the garlic in the salt with the coriander seeds and mix with the remainder of the marinade ingredients.

Put the lamb into a large china or glass bowl and pour the marinade over, turning and coating the pieces of meat. Cover with foil and leave in a cool place for 3–6 hours. Turn the meat from time to time.

Tip the meat and every drop of the marinade into a saucepan. Place over a high heat, cover and bring up to the boil. Cook briskly for a few minutes to seal the lamb and concentrate the flavours. Reduce the heat to low, add just enough hot stock with the tomato paste so that the meat is not entirely immersed in liquid. If the onion is hand-chopped, the marinade will be less liquid and it may be necessary to add a little more stock. Cover the pan and simmer for 1 hour. If you cook this in advance, cool uncovered and store in the refrigerator with a double wrapping of foil. Allow 30 minutes for reheating, which should be gentle.

Serves 8

---

230 calories per serving

Lemon-minted roast lamb

1.6-kg ($3\frac{1}{2}$-lb) leg of lamb
10 coriander seeds
2.5 ml ($\frac{1}{2}$ level tsp) whole black
    peppercorns
2 cloves garlic, skinned
5 ml (1 level tsp) salt
30 ml (2 tbsp) finely chopped fresh
    mint

a few sprigs mint
finely grated rind and juice of 1 large
    lemon
60 ml (4 tbsp) cold water
100 ml (4 fl oz) dry white wine or
    150 ml ($\frac{1}{4}$ pint) boiling water

Prepare the lamb 2–3 hours before cooking, so that the flavours are absorbed by the meat. Shave off some of the surplus fat. Cut 12 small slits about 1 cm (½ in) deep into the lamb. Crush together the coriander seeds, peppercorns and garlic mixed with the salt. Add half the chopped mint and lemon rind. Work the pounded ingredients into the incisions, rubbing any surplus over the meat. Sprinkle with the lemon juice and the rest of the chopped mint.

Stand a rack in the roasting pan or dish. Add the sprigs of mint and lay the lamb on them. Add 60 ml (4 tbsp) cold water to the pan. Cook in the centre of the oven at 180°C (350°F) mark 4 for 1½ hours, or a little less if you like your lamb pink, as I do. Baste once after 30 minutes cooking. Roast for another 30 minutes, then skim off any fat in the pan. Pour in the wine or boiling water, mixing it with the pan juices, then baste the meat again. Return to the oven to complete cooking. Remove the joint to a heated platter and keep warm in the turned off oven while making the gravy. Pour the pan juices into a small saucepan, scraping up the sediment for maximum flavour. Gently bring to the boil and adjust seasoning.

Serves 8

---

270 calories per 100-g (4-oz) serving

Spiced leg of lamb

Illustrated in colour facing page 76

The spicy aroma which comes from this dish when cooking is mouthwatering.

1.4-kg (3-lb) leg of lamb	the seeds of 2 cardamom pods
5 ml (1 level tsp) salt	2 cloves garlic, skinned
2.5 ml (½ level tsp) freshly ground	finely grated rind and juice of
black pepper or 1.25 ml (¼ level tsp)	1 medium orange
powder	60 ml (4 tbsp) cold water
5 ml (1 level tsp) coriander seeds	orange and watercress sprigs to
1.25 ml (¼ level tsp) cumin seeds	garnish

Prepare the lamb several hours in advance of cooking time so that the flavours are fully absorbed by the meat. Shave off some of the surplus fat. Cut 12 small slits about 1 cm (½ in) deep into the lamb. Rub the salt and pepper all over the surface.

Crush together the coriander, cumin, cardamom seeds and garlic. Add the orange rind and 5 ml (1 tsp) juice and work to a paste. Push this paste well into the incisions. Any surplus should be rubbed over the meat. Sprinkle with half the orange juice.

Stand the meat on a rack in a roasting pan or dish, pour the water into the pan and spoon the rest of the orange juice over the lamb. Cook in the centre of the oven at 180°C (350°F) mark 4 for 40 minutes *without basting*. Pour away any surplus fat which has dripped into the pan. If the water has evaporated add a little more to the pan – about 45–60 ml (3–4 tbsp).

Increase the heat to 190°C (375°F) mark 5 and roast for another 45 minutes, giving a total cooking time of 1 hour 25 minutes. The meat should be just pink around the bone. Use the pan juices and the natural meat juices for gravy. Add a little more orange juice and rind for extra flavour. Leek and swede purée (see page 90), courgettes and carrots all go well with this dish.

Serves 6–8

270 calories per 100-g (4-oz) serving
plus 100 g (4 oz) carrots – 20 calories
100 g (4 oz) courgettes – 12 calories

Pork parcels

350 g (12 oz) onions, skinned
100 g (4 oz) cooking apple
5 ml (1 tsp) oil
10 ml (2 tsp) Worcestershire sauce
8–10 twists of pepper from a mill or
    1.25 ml (¼ level tsp) powder
2.5 ml (½ level tsp) salt
6 100-g (4-oz) slices of pork fillet,
    trimmed of visible fat
15 ml (1 level tbsp) smooth French
    mustard
2.5 ml (½ level tsp) powdered
    rosemary

15 g (½ oz) flour mixed with 1.25 ml
    (¼ level tsp) salt, 1.25 ml (¼ level tsp)
    freshly ground pepper and 2.5 ml
    (½ level tsp) sweet paprika pepper
100 ml (4 fl oz) dry white wine
250 ml (scant ½ pint) stock made by
    using ½ beef stock cube and 10 ml
    (2 level tsp) tomato paste
1 bay leaf
1 clove
strip of lemon peel
sprig of parsley
1 small red pepper

Chop the onions and apple as finely as possible. Heat the oil in a wide heavy-based saucepan. Add the onions and apple, cover the pan and cook gently for about 15 minutes, until they are soft. Stir and turn them once or twice. Sprinkle with the Worcestershire sauce, pepper and salt. The onion and apple mixture should be thick. Uncover and cool slightly. You will need about half for the stuffing and the remainder will flavour the sauce.

Flatten the pork slices on a board to roughly 7.5 by 12.5 cm (3 by 5 in). Spread with mustard, a pinch of rosemary and a little seasoning. Place 10 ml (2 tsp) onion and apple mixture on each fillet slice. Roll up into neat parcels and tie with fine string. Roll them in the seasoned flour. Lay the pork parcels on the remaining onion and apple mixture, pour in the wine and bring rapidly to the boil. Cover and bubble for 2 minutes. Pour in the boiling stock and, keeping the heat moderate, cook covered for another 5 minutes. Reduce the heat. The pork parcels will seal in the steam and boiling liquid. Add the bay leaf, clove, lemon peel and parsley sprig. Stir well to loosen any sediment at the bottom of the pan. Cover and simmer very gently for about 45 minutes until tender.

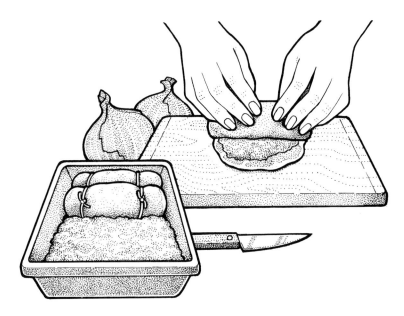

Rolling slices of pork over an apple and onion filling to make pork parcels

Remove the core and seeds from the red pepper and cut into thin strips. Stir into the sauce 10 minutes before serving. Check the seasoning. To serve, remove meat to a shallow dish and cut off the strings. Pour some of the sauce over the meat and serve the rest separately, making sure it is very hot.

Note Cucumber makes an attractive alternative to red pepper. Half a medium cucumber should be sufficient. Peel and cut it in half lengthways, then into quarters. Remove most of the seeds and cut into 2.5-cm (1-in) pieces. Add them to the hot liquid 5–10 minutes before serving. The shorter cooking time is recommended if you enjoy a crisp vegetable.

Serves 6

200 calories per serving

'Leanline' boneless roast loin of pork

The traditional method of roasting pork is usually too fatty and high in calories for dieters. However, there is a 'Leanline' alternative which eliminates surplus fat without diminishing flavour. I use a boned and rolled loin of pork with the rind removed so that fat can be reduced to a thin layer, say 0.5 cm ($\frac{1}{4}$ in) at the most. Generally butchers are most helpful and will prepare the joint for you.

The flavour of pork is greatly improved if it is marinated for some hours before cooking. The marinade may be a dry mixture of herbs and spices or one containing wine, vinegar or lemon juice. Even rubbing salt and pepper all over the joint is effective. Long, slow roasting of marinated pork produces tender moist meat. It is particularly delicious cold, so leftovers provide an unusually good meal.

1.4-kg (3-lb) lean loin of pork, rind removed, boned and rolled
1 clove garlic, skinned
150 ml ($\frac{1}{4}$ pint) stock

For the marinade
the seeds of 1 cardamom pod
3 juniper berries
5 ml (1 tsp) finely chopped fresh or 2.5 ml ($\frac{1}{2}$ tsp) dried sage

2 bay leaves, broken into small pieces
15 ml (1 tbsp) finely chopped parsley
5 ml (1 level tsp) salt
2.5 ml ($\frac{1}{2}$ level tsp) freshly ground pepper or 1.25 ml ($\frac{1}{4}$ level tsp) powder
juice of 1 lemon or about 30 ml (2 tbsp) bottled juice

Untie the pork. Shave away all but a thin layer of covering fat and remove any underside fat. Push slivers of garlic into the meat, making small incisions where necessary.

To prepare the marinade, open the cardamom pod with the point of a sharp knife and crush the seeds together with the juniper berries. In a small bowl, mix together with all the dry ingredients and herbs. Rub this dry marinade all over the pork, place it in a non-corrosive dish (enamel-lined, glass or stainless steel) and pour over the lemon juice. Cover loosely with foil and leave in a cool place for at least 3 hours, for the meat to absorb the flavours. Turn the meat a few times.

Remove the meat, dry slightly and tie with string into a neat shape. Place the joint on a rack in a roasting pan or dish and spoon the remaining lemon marinade juice over it. Cook in the centre of the oven at 170°C (325°F) mark 2–3 for 1$\frac{3}{4}$–2 hours. Baste during cooking. Cooking is complete when the juices run clear; if slightly pink, a little more cooking is necessary. Remove the joint to a heated platter or suitable dish. To make the sauce, pour away any fat from the roasting pan. Pour in 150 ml ($\frac{1}{4}$ pint) hot stock and bring to the boil. Scrape the bottom of the tin to dissolve some of the caramelised juices. Taste and adjust seasoning and pour into a heated sauce jug. Wine-braised red cabbage (see page 88) is a perfect accompaniment.

Serves 8

330 calories per 100-g (4-oz) serving

Aromatic pork and beef meatballs

For the spiced meat mixture

450 g (1 lb) lean pork
225 g (8 oz) lean beef
1 medium onion, skinned
5 ml (1 level tsp) cinnamon
2.5 ml ($\frac{1}{2}$ level tsp) ground ginger
2.5 ml ($\frac{1}{2}$ level tsp) cumin seeds
the seeds of 1 cardamom pod
1.25 ml ($\frac{1}{4}$ level tsp) nutmeg
5 ml (1 level tsp) salt
6–8 twists of pepper from a mill or
   good pinch powder
1 clove garlic, skinned and crushed
about 15 ml (1 tbsp) lemon juice

100 g (4 oz) carrot, peeled and grated
100 g (4 oz) turnip, peeled and grated
1 stick celery with leaves, finely
   chopped
600 ml (1 pint) chicken stock made up
   using 1 chicken stock cube and
   15 ml (1 tbsp) tomato paste
1 bay leaf
few parsley stalks
strip of lemon rind

If you mince the meat yourself, add the onion at the same time. If minced meat is bought, the onion should be grated or very finely chopped.

In a large bowl mix together the meat, onion, crushed spices, seasonings and crushed garlic. Using an electric beater or wooden spoon, thoroughly beat the mixture until a smooth, pasty texture is obtained, working in the lemon juice to moisten. Leave in a cool place for 30 minutes or so to absorb flavours. With wetted hands, roll into medium-sized balls – allow two or three per serving.

Place the prepared vegetables in a wide, heavy-based saucepan. Lay the meatballs on top. Pour in the hot stock, add the bay leaf, parsley stalks and strip of lemon rind. Cover the pan, place over a brisk heat and bring to the boil. Reduce the heat to low and cook at a lazy simmer for 1 hour. Check the seasoning. To skim the fat, allow to cool for 5 minutes and spoon off all visible fat. If time permits, use the cold skimming method (see page 54).
Note This dish freezes well.
Serves 6

210 calories per serving

'Leanline' leftovers in a light curry sauce

There is nothing more disheartening than the remains of a cold joint or chicken, usually not quite enough to make a meal. However, a well flavoured sauce will transform leftovers into a tempting spicy dish. This sauce may be made in advance, covered and refrigerated for up to 3 days, or you can keep a supply in the freezer so that an easy meal can quickly be made.

1 small onion, skinned
1 small carrot, peeled
1 medium stick celery with leaves
100 g (4 oz) mushrooms
25 g (1 oz) low fat spread
5–10 ml (1–2 level tsp) mild curry
   powder

15 g ($\frac{1}{2}$ oz) flour, wholemeal
   preferably
150 ml ($\frac{1}{4}$ pint) chicken stock made up
   using $\frac{1}{4}$ chicken stock cube
150 ml ($\frac{1}{4}$ pint) skimmed milk
2.5 ml ($\frac{1}{2}$ level tsp) dried oregano

Remember that the meat will have been seasoned when first cooked, therefore check the seasoning after the meat or chicken has been gently heated in the sauce, adding a very little salt and pepper if necessary.

Finely chop the onion, carrot and celery with its leaves. Wash the mushrooms quickly in cold water. Drain and dry on kitchen paper. Cut into thin slices, including stalks. Melt the fat over a low heat then increase it slightly. Tip in the chopped vegetables, not the mushrooms, and cook for 5 minutes without browning. Reduce the heat. Sprinkle in the curry powder and cook for 2 minutes to eliminate the raw taste. Add the flour, working it well into the fat, and cook again for another minute.

Gradually stir in the hot stock, keeping the mixture smooth, and then stir in the skimmed milk. Increase the heat to moderate, bring to the boil, tip in the sliced mushrooms, including stalks, and add oregano. Reduce the heat to very low, cover and simmer gently for 20 minutes. On no account should this sauce *boil*. If necessary, partially cover with a lid to maintain a gentle simmer.

Add the meat or chicken, cut into small pieces (about 450 g (1 lb) for 4 servings), and heat, very gently indeed, for a further 20 minutes. Crisply cooked Lemony cabbage (see page 87) is particularly good with this sauce.

Serves 4

260 calories for the sauce recipe

Poultry

Chicken is economical in cost and in calories. It has therefore become commonplace, and imagination is needed to avoid monotony.

Ordinary roast chicken can be made interesting by flavouring with herbs and spices and by using the giblets to enrich the gravy. Nothing need be wasted, as the carcass, with the addition of vegetables, herbs and seasonings, can be transformed into stock (see page 20). Spicy marinades replace butter and oil. The poultry absorbs the flavours and is then grilled or cooked in the oven.

Casseroled chicken, skilfully enhanced with mushrooms, dried fruit, stock or wine, becomes ideal dinner party fare.

Mushroom'd chicken

1.6-kg ($3\frac{1}{2}$-lb) chicken and the giblets
175 g (6 oz) mushrooms
1 clove garlic, skinned
2.5 ml ($\frac{1}{2}$ level tsp) salt
15 ml (1 tbsp) natural yogurt
12 twists of pepper from a mill or
   1.25 ml ($\frac{1}{4}$ level tsp) powder
1 lemon

5 ml (1 level tsp) salt
5 ml (1 level tsp) dried tarragon
150 ml ($\frac{1}{4}$ pint) home made chicken
   stock or make up using $\frac{1}{4}$ chicken
   stock cube with 1 small onion,
   sliced, and 1 carrot, sliced
15 ml (1 tbsp) chopped fresh parsley

Untruss the chicken, remove the giblets and wash them in a bowl of cold water. Dry on kitchen paper and snip away any greenish-looking flesh. Set aside. Cut the liver into small pieces. Wipe the chicken inside and out.

Wash the mushrooms quickly in cold water, rubbing away any dirt between the fingers. Drain and dry on kitchen paper. Break off the stalks and chop them coarsely – the mushroom caps should be left whole. Crush the garlic in the salt and stir into the yogurt together with the mushroom stalks and pieces of liver. Add several twists of pepper from a mill. Squeeze the lemon – don't throw the halves away.

Working with fingertips and thumbs, loosen the skin of the chicken and lift it away from the breast, sliding the fingers between the skin and flesh. This is a fairly easy manoeuvre but a gentle touch is necessary. Snip the membrane which adheres to the breastbone. Slide the mushroom caps under the skin until the whole of the breast is covered. Although the surface may look a little bumpy, it will remain intact. Rub the whole surface of the bird with the salt and pepper and spoon the yogurt mixture into the cavity. Push in the squeezed lemon halves. Tuck in the loose flap of neck skin and tie the legs loosely with a piece of string. Place the chicken on its side in a suitable roasting pan or dish – it shouldn't be too large – sprinkle with the dried tarragon and lemon juice. Add the giblets and pour in the stock. (If using the stock cube method, put the sliced onion and carrot in the pan to improve the flavour.)

Place in the centre of the oven at 190°C (375°F) mark 5 and allow a total cooking time of 1 hour 20 minutes. Baste after the first 30 minutes, roast for another 30 minutes, and then turn the bird on to its back. Baste again, spooning the juices over the breast and legs. Increase the heat slightly to 200°C (400°F) mark 6 for the last 20 minutes, so that the bird becomes a rich golden brown. Remove to a hot serving dish and keep warm.

Strain the juices into a small saucepan, stir in the chopped parsley and boil for 3 minutes, uncovered, to reduce and concentrate the flavour. Carve the chicken into serving portions and moisten with a little of the hot sauce. Pour the rest into a warmed jug or sauceboat.

Serves 6

---

240 calories per 175-g (6-oz) serving

Boned apricot chicken

1.8-kg (4-lb) chicken, boned
salt and freshly ground pepper (see method)

For the stuffing
100 g (4 oz) dried apricots, soaked overnight
30 ml (2 tbsp) dry vermouth
5 ml (1 level tsp) powdered rosemary
5 ml (1 level tsp) ground turmeric
1 clove garlic, skinned
15 g ($\frac{1}{2}$ oz) butter
50 g (2 oz) long grain rice, washed and soaked for 1 hour in cold water
2.5 ml ($\frac{1}{2}$ level tsp) salt
2.5 ml ($\frac{1}{2}$ level tsp) freshly ground pepper or 1.25 ml ($\frac{1}{4}$ level tsp) powder
2.5 ml ($\frac{1}{2}$ level tsp) mild curry powder

5 ml (1 tsp) oil
50 g (2 oz) onion, skinned and finely chopped
50 g (2 oz) mushrooms, cleaned and finely chopped

For the sauce
100 g (4 oz) onions, skinned and chopped
100 g (4 oz) carrots, peeled and chopped
175 g (6 oz) flat mushrooms, cleaned and thinly sliced
2 tomatoes, skinned
100 ml (4 fl oz) dry white wine
150 ml ($\frac{1}{4}$ pint) home made chicken stock or make up using $\frac{1}{4}$ chicken stock cube
30 ml (2 tbsp) single cream

To prepare the stuffing, drain the apricots and pat dry on kitchen paper. Halve them and place in a bowl. Sprinkle with the dry vermouth, rosemary and turmeric. Leave for 1 hour

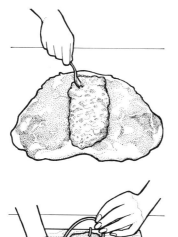

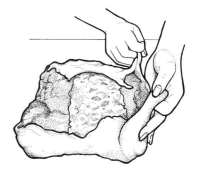

1. Spooning stuffing into the boned chicken
2. Reshaping the chicken by folding the sides over the stuffing
3. Using fine string to sew up the stuffed bird

to absorb flavours. Crush the garlic in a little salt and blend with the butter. Drain the rice and cook in plenty of boiling salted water for exactly 11 minutes. Drain and cool. Tip the cooked rice into a large bowl and mix with the salt, pepper and curry powder.

Brush a non-stick pan with the oil and place over a low heat. Leave a few seconds before adding the onion and mushrooms. Stir and allow to soften for 5–10 minutes. Tip them into the seasoned rice with the garlic butter. Gently stir the apricots and juices into the rice mixture.

Lay the chicken flat on a board and rub the inside with salt and pepper. Pile the stuffing along the centre of the bird. Re-shape the chicken by easing the sides up and over the stuffing. Sew up the openings with fine string. Tuck the loose neck skin under the back of the bird. Rub the skin with salt, pepper and powdered rosemary. Turn the bird on to its back and re-shape if necessary.

Place the prepared onion, carrot, mushroom and chopped tomato flesh over the base of a flameproof casserole just large enough to hold the chicken. Place the stuffed bird on the bed of vegetables. Pour in the wine and cover. Place over moderately high heat, bring to the boil and bubble for 5 minutes. Remove to the centre of the oven at 220°C (425°F) mark 7 and cook for 1 hour. Check half way through cooking. If the skin is well browned reduce the heat to 200°C (400°F) mark 6.

Transfer the chicken to a heated serving dish and leave in a warm oven. Pour the contents of the casserole into a small saucepan, place over a medium heat, add the 150 ml

($\frac{1}{4}$ pint) chicken stock and bubble hard for 5 minutes to reduce and concentrate the flavour. Taste and adjust the seasoning. Stir in the cream. Remove the string from the bird, pour over a little of the sauce and surround with vegetables. Put the rest of the sauce in a heated jug. Serve with a little extra rice, crisp beansprouts (fresh or canned) and carrots.

To cook fresh beansprouts, wash in cold water and drain. Cook for 3 minutes in boiling stock or water containing 2.5 ml ($\frac{1}{2}$ level tsp) salt and 10 ml (2 tsp lemon juice).
Serves 6

260 calories per serving
plus 50 g (2 oz) boiled rice – 70 calories
25 g (1 oz) beansprouts – 8 calories
100 g (4 oz) cooked carrots – 20 calories

Orange roasted chicken

1.6-kg (3$\frac{1}{2}$-lb) chicken and the giblets
5 ml (1 level tsp) salt
2.5 ml ($\frac{1}{2}$ level tsp) freshly ground
   black pepper or 1.25 ml ($\frac{1}{4}$ level tsp)
   powder
2.5 ml ($\frac{1}{2}$ level tsp) sweet paprika
   pepper

175 g (6 oz) onions, skinned
1 large orange
150 ml ($\frac{1}{4}$ pint) boiling water
50 ml (2 fl oz) dry vermouth
   (optional)

Untruss the chicken, remove the giblets and wash them in a bowl of cold water. Dry on kitchen paper and snip away any greenish-looking flesh. Cut into pieces and set aside. Wipe the chicken and rub inside and out with salt, pepper and paprika. Thinly slice the onions and lay them in a roasting pan or dish just large enough to hold the chicken and giblets.

Squeeze the orange. Cut the squeezed halves into quarters and push them inside the chicken – two or three pieces in the cavity and one at the neck end under the loose skin. Place the chicken on its side, or upside down, in the pan. Sprinkle with the orange juice. Put the chopped giblets round the chicken. Pour in the boiling water.

Place in the centre of the oven at 190°C (375°F) mark 5 and allow a total cooking time of 1 hour 20 minutes. Baste after 30 minutes, then roast for another 30 minutes. Turn the bird over on to its back and baste again, spooning the juices over the breast and legs. Increase the heat slightly to 200°C (400°F) mark 6 for the last 20 minutes so that the bird becomes a rich golden brown.

The pan juices will supply all the gravy you need. Reheat with the onions and giblets, stirring in the dry vermouth if used.
Serves 6

240 calories per 175-g (6-oz) serving
plus 50 ml (2 fl oz) dry vermouth – 68 calories

Rosemary roasted chicken

1.4-kg (3-lb) chicken and the giblets
5 ml (1 level tsp) powdered rosemary
5 ml (1 level tsp) salt
2.5 ml ($\frac{1}{2}$ level tsp) freshly ground
 pepper or 1.25 ml ($\frac{1}{4}$ level tsp)
 powder

1 large lemon
1 clove garlic, skinned
10 ml (2 tsp) oil

If possible prepare 1–2 hours before cooking so the flavours are thoroughly absorbed.

Wash the giblets and cut away any greenish looking flesh. Dry them on kitchen paper and leave on one side. Wipe the chicken inside and out. Mix together the rosemary, salt and pepper and rub this all over the bird including a little inside. Squeeze the lemon and put the squeezed halves and the garlic clove inside the cavity.

Lay the bird upside down in a roasting pan or dish together with the giblets, but not the liver. Sprinkle with the lemon juice and oil. Place in the centre of the oven at 190°C (375°F) mark 5 and cook for 45 minutes *without* basting. Then turn the chicken on to its back, breast side uppermost, and baste with the juices. Add the liver to the pan and cook for another 30 minutes – 1$\frac{1}{4}$ hours total cooking time. Increase the heat for the last 15 minutes to 200°C (400°F) mark 6. The chicken will now be a rich golden brown in colour. The chicken is cooked when the juice from the leg runs clear and not when the flesh is falling off the bones! The flesh remains succulent and is delicious hot or cold.

The pan juices provide a delicious lemony sauce. Add the chopped giblets, including the liver to the drained juices. Reheat and serve separately in a sauceboat or jug.
Serves 6

---

250 calories per 175-g (6-oz) serving

Mustard marinated chicken

This dish should be prepared several hours before cooking. It may be covered and left in a cool place during the day or overnight in the refrigerator. Remove the foil and leave at room temperature for 2 hours so that the flavours mellow before placing in the oven.

1.4-kg (3-lb) chicken, cut into 6 pieces,
 or bought chicken portions

For the marinade
15 ml (1 level tbsp) smooth French
 mustard, preferably Dijon
60 ml (4 tbsp) natural yogurt
15 ml (1 tbsp) lemon juice

5 ml (1 level tsp) turmeric powder
1.25 ml ($\frac{1}{4}$ level tsp) ground ginger
1 clove garlic, skinned and crushed
100 g (4 oz) onion, skinned and thinly
 sliced
5 ml (1 level tsp) salt
12 twists of pepper from a mill or
 1.25 ml ($\frac{1}{4}$ level tsp) powder

76

*Spiced leg of lamb (page 65), 'Leanline' baked
potato halves (page 86), Leek and swede purée (page 90)* ▶

Wipe the chicken inside and out. Dry it with a clean tea towel or kitchen paper. Cut into portions using a sharp knife and scissors. It is important that frozen chicken is thoroughly drained and dried before attempting to cut or cook it. Trim away loose flaps of skin, visible fat and any greenish-looking bones and flesh from inside the bird. Giblets, wing tips and trimmed small bones can be used to make stock. Freeze the liver.

Mix together all the marinade ingredients. Cut one or two small slits in each chicken portion and place them in a shallow ovenproof dish or enamelled roasting pan. Spoon over the marinade, making sure that every piece is coated. Cover the dish with foil and marinate for at least 3 hours. A double covering is necessary for refrigerating. Turn the pieces once or twice during the marinating period, and again when the foil is removed for the couple of hours before cooking (see recipe introduction).

Place the chicken in the centre of the oven at 190°C (375°F) mark 5 and cook for $1-1\frac{1}{4}$ hours depending on the size of chicken portions. Turn the pieces half way through cooking. The chicken will absorb some of the marinade but there should be sufficient sauce. Oven temperatures may vary slightly so reduce the heat to 180° C (350°F) mark 4 if your oven seems rather hot.

Overcooked chicken flesh is dry and unpalatable no matter how much liquid is added. Test with the tip of a sharp knife at the top of the leg bone. Clear juices indicate that it is fully cooked. Serve Mustard marinated chicken with lightly cooked runner beans or with broccoli.
Serves 6

---

200 calories per serving
plus 100 g (4 oz) lightly cooked runner beans – 10 calories
100 g (4 oz) broccoli – 15 calories

Rosy chicken

Illustrated in colour on the jacket

**1.4-kg (3-lb) chicken, cut into
6 pieces, or bought chicken
portions**
**10 ml (2 level tsp) sweet paprika
pepper**
5 ml (1 level tsp) salt
**1.25 ml ($\frac{1}{4}$ level tsp) freshly ground
pepper or good pinch powder**
175 g (6 oz) red pepper
100 g (4 oz) onions, skinned
100 g (4 oz) carrots, peeled

15 ml (1 tbsp) red wine vinegar
1 bay leaf
2 drops Tabasco pepper sauce
1 sprig parsley
**397-g (14-oz) can Italian tomatoes,
lightly crushed**
10 ml (2 level tsp) cornflour
30 ml (2 level tbsp) natural yogurt

Jerusalem artichoke and carrot purée (page 89),
◄ *Reviving winter crunchy salad (page 93),*
'Leanline' ratatouille (page 84)

Prepare the chicken following instructions given in the first paragraph of Mustard marinated chicken on page 77.

Rub the chicken pieces with 5 ml (1 level tsp) paprika, salt and pepper. Cut the red pepper in half, deseed and cut away thick stalks and the core. Slice or chop finely. Finely chop or slice the onion and carrot, or chop in a blender, adding the vinegar. Do not overblend or the mixture will become too liquid.

Place the prepared vegetables with vinegar in a heavy-based shallow saucepan. Lay the chicken pieces on top, cover the pan and rapidly bring to the boil. Cook over high heat for 8–10 minutes. The steam will seal the chicken. Reduce heat. Add the bay leaf, Tabasco sauce, parsley sprig and the canned tomatoes with juice. The liquid should come two-thirds up the side of the chicken. Cover the pan and simmer for 30 minutes.

In a small bowl, mix together the cornflour, 5 ml (1 level tsp) paprika and yogurt. Stir this into the hot cooking juices and simmer for 5 minutes.
Serves 6

---

220 calories per serving

'Leanline' gourmet chicken

1.4-kg (3-lb) chicken, cut into quarters
1 clove garlic, skinned
2.5 ml ($\frac{1}{2}$ level tsp) salt
8–10 twists of pepper from a mill or good pinch powder
a little nutmeg
2.5 ml ($\frac{1}{2}$ level tsp) powdered rosemary
15 g ($\frac{1}{2}$ oz) plain flour
50 g (2 oz) dried apricots, soaked overnight
30 ml (2 tbsp) dry sherry
100 g (4 oz) mushrooms
50 g (2 oz) onion, skinned
50 g (2 oz) carrot, peeled
225 g (8 oz) tomatoes, skinned
15 g ($\frac{1}{2}$ oz) butter
5 ml (1 level tsp) mild curry powder
150 ml ($\frac{1}{4}$ pint) home made chicken stock or make up using $\frac{1}{4}$ chicken stock cube
finely chopped parsley to garnish

Trim away loose flaps of chicken skin and remove visible fat. Dry the chicken portions. Crush the garlic in the salt, mix with the pepper, nutmeg and rosemary then rub it all over the chicken pieces. Sprinkle with the flour.

Drain the dried apricots and scissor-snip into strips. Sprinkle with the sherry. Wash the mushrooms quickly in cold water. Drain, dry on kitchen paper and chop into small pieces. Finely chop the onion and carrot. Coarsely chop the tomatoes.

A shallow flameproof casserole is ideal for this dish but it may be cooked on top of the cooker in a saucepan. Melt the butter over a low heat. Add the chopped vegetables, mushrooms and tomatoes, and sprinkle in the curry powder. Raise the heat to medium and cook for 1 minute, working in the curry powder. Lay the chicken pieces on the vegetables and add the apricots, sherry and stock. Cover the pan with foil then the lid. Keeping the heat fairly high, bubble the contents for 5 minutes. Reduce the heat. Continue to cook on top of the cooker for a further 30 minutes, or place in the centre of the oven at 180°C (350°F) mark 4 for the same length of time.

To serve, remove the chicken pieces to a heated shallow ovenproof dish. Liquidise half the vegetables in an electric blender, reheat and serve separately in a sauceboat or jug. Spoon the remaining vegetables over the chicken with any juices from the pan. Sprinkle with finely chopped parsley. Serve with boiled rice, baked tomato halves and peas.

Serves 4

---

305 calories per serving
plus 50 g (2 oz) boiled rice – 70 calories
50 g (2 oz) baked tomato halves – 10 calories
100 g (4 oz) peas – 55 calories

'Leanline' devilled chicken

In spite of the term 'devilled' this dish is aromatic rather than fiery.

1.4-kg (3-lb) chicken or 6 chicken legs or portions

For the devil sauce
20 ml (4 level tsp) strong smooth French mustard
15 ml (1 level tbsp) tomato ketchup
10 ml (2 tsp) Worcestershire sauce
50 g (2 oz) onion, finely chopped
2.5 ml ($\frac{1}{2}$ level tsp) cinnamon

2.5 ml ($\frac{1}{2}$ level tsp) sweet paprika pepper
2.5 ml ($\frac{1}{2}$ level tsp) dried thyme
2.5 ml ($\frac{1}{2}$ level tsp) salt
6 twists of pepper from a mill or good pinch powder
1.25 ml ($\frac{1}{4}$ level tsp) nutmeg
15–30 ml (1–2 tbsp) natural yogurt
15 g ($\frac{1}{2}$ oz) stale wholemeal breadcrumbs, slightly dried

Wipe the chicken inside and out and dry it thoroughly with a clean tea towel. Using a sharp knife and scissors, cut it into 6 portions, or quarters for larger servings. Trim away loose flaps of skin and remove visible fat. Snip off greenish-looking bones or flesh inside the bird. Giblets, wing tips and trimmed bones will make good stock or soup. Freeze the liver, or grill it with the chicken for a few minutes. Make one or two shallow cuts in the thickest part of the legs.

Blend all the devil sauce ingredients together except the yogurt, which should be gradually worked in, 15 ml (1 tbsp) at a time, until you have a thick creamy sauce. Coat the chicken pieces on both sides with the sauce. Reserve a little of the sauce for basting later. Leave in a cool place for 1 hour for the flavours to develop.

Pre-heat the grill to moderately hot. Place the chicken pieces, underside up, in the grill pan, not on the rack, making sure they are well coated with the sauce. The surface of the chicken should be 12.5–15 cm (5–6 in) below the flame. Grill for 10 minutes, basting after

5 minutes. Turn the pieces over and baste with a little of the spare sauce mixture. Grill for a further 5–10 minutes, depending on the size of the portions and the thickness of the flesh.

Spoon the remaining sauce over the browned chicken. Scatter with the breadcrumbs. Increase the heat and cook the chicken carefully for 5 minutes to brown and crisp the surface. Any hot sauce in the grill pan should be served with the chicken.

To test when the chicken is cooked, pierce the thickest part of the leg with the point of a sharp knife or skewer. The juices which flow out should be colourless. Large chicken pieces may need a few minutes longer, but keep the heat moderate and the flesh will remain moist. Serve with lightly cooked green vegetables and brown rice.

Serves 6

200 calories per 225-g (8-oz) raw chicken portion

Chicken in a mushroom and vermouth sauce

It is worth storing or freezing half a roasted chicken just to make this dish. I use the same sauce for cooked turkey. It freezes on its own and is one of my favourite freezer standbys.

½ roasted chicken
50 g (2 oz) onion, skinned
50 g (2 oz) carrot, peeled
25 g (1 oz) lean ham
100 g (4 oz) mushrooms
15 g (½ oz) butter

15 g (½ oz) wholemeal flour
30 ml (2 tbsp) dry vermouth
150 ml (¼ pint) home made chicken stock or make up using ¼ chicken stock cube
salt and freshly ground pepper

Cut the chicken flesh into small chunks including some of the browned skin. Reserve a few small bones, thigh and wing, to add to the sauce.

Finely chop the onion, carrot and ham. Wash the mushrooms quickly in cold water. Drain, dry on kitchen paper and chop into small pieces. Melt the butter over a how heat, stir in the onion, carrot and ham. Raise the heat to moderate, cover and cook for 5 minutes. Add the mushrooms and cook for 2 minutes.

Sprinkle in the flour, working it into the vegetables; cook for another minute. Pour in the vermouth which will bubble, reduce the heat and stir in the hot stock. Partially cover the pan and maintain the sauce at a lazy simmer for 5 minutes. Add the chicken chunks, bones and skin. Cover, or partially cover with lid, and gently simmer for 15–20 minutes. Remove the bones with a perforated spoon.

As the chicken has already been seasoned and the sauce will absorb some of its flavours, very little salt and pepper should be added before putting in the chicken. (The ham, too, gives a certain amount of salt.) Check the seasoning 5 minutes before serving.

Serves 4

270 calories per 100-g (4-oz) serving

Vegetable dishes
and salads

Fresh vegetables in season always deserve careful preparation. Most vegetables, especially the new crop, can be eaten raw and make the most delightful salads. All they require is a little lemon juice or a light yogurt-based dressing to complement the flavour.

The tendency to overcook vegetables is very common, and to keep cooked green vegetables warm for more than a few minutes destroys the taste as well as the nutrients. Most green vegetables benefit from a brief cooking in a large saucepan containing lightly salted boiling water. New carrots, turnips and courgettes are delicious cooked in chicken stock.

Choose vegetables with care and avoid any that are wilted, bruised or flabby. If possible, store them in the refrigerator or in a cool larder. Be adventurous and try the less popular varieties, such as Jerusalem artichokes, celeriac, chicory, kohlrabi – not forgetting the under-used swede, red cabbage and, of course, spinach.

I have included recipes for everyday vegetables, like cabbage and leeks, as well as interesting purées. The salads indicate the endless possibilities of raw vegetables.

Regard vegetables as a food rather than a filler and give them the attention they deserve.

Braised leeks

Illustrated in colour facing page 45

450 g (1 lb) leeks
50 g (2 oz) carrot, peeled
15 g ($\frac{1}{2}$ oz) butter
salt and freshly ground pepper

10 ml (2 tsp) lemon juice
5 ml (1 tsp) Worcestershire sauce
2 tomatoes, skinned and sliced

Cut off the roots and the coarse dark green part of the leek stalk. Make a 7.5–10 cm (3–4 in) long cut through the centre of the leeks at the green end. Turn and make a second cut so that the last few inches of the green stalk opens into four quarters. Hold the leeks under running cold water to remove as much grit as possible. Soak them, cut ends down, in a jug of cold salted water, using 5 ml (1 level tsp) salt, for several hours. Most of the dirt will be drawn into the water.

Remove the leeks and drain. Cut into 1-cm ($\frac{1}{2}$-in) slices. Obstinate gritty pieces should be rinsed under cold running water. Dry on kitchen paper. Slice or dice the carrot. Melt the butter over a low heat in a wide heavy-bottomed pan. Add the carrot and stir in the leeks, turning them over so that they are coated with the butter. Cover the pan and cook the vegetables gently for 10 minutes until barely tender. Sprinkle with a little salt and freshly ground pepper, the lemon juice and Worcestershire sauce. Add the tomatoes. Cover and

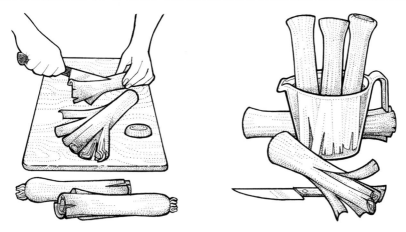

*1. Slicing through the centre of a leek to divide the dark green
part of the stalk into four quarters*
2. Soaking leeks, cut end down, in a jug of cold salted water

cook for 2–3 minutes, just long enough for the tomatoes to become hot, before serving. The tomato slices should remain whole and firm. Braised leeks are excellent with all fish dishes.

Serves 4

65 calories per serving

Stirred mushrooms

225 g (8 oz) mushrooms
2 spring onions
1 clove garlic, skinned
10 ml (2 tsp) oil (olive oil preferred)

pinch salt
4–5 twists of pepper from a mill or
  pinch powder

Wash the mushrooms quickly in cold water. Drain and dry on kitchen paper. Cut into slices including the stalks. Trim and clean the spring onions and cut into 2.5-cm (1-in) lengths. Chop the garlic finely.

Heat the oil over a medium heat in a heavy-based frying pan, large enough to cook the mushrooms without crowding. Fry the garlic until it is lightly coloured. It must not burn or become too brown. Add the onions and mushrooms and increase the heat slightly. Stir and turn the mushrooms so that they cook quickly – about 3 minutes. Season with the salt and pepper and serve immediately.

Stirred mushrooms are particularly good with eggs or grilled fish.

15 calories per 50-g (2-oz) serving

'Leanline' ratatouille

Illustrated in colour facing page 77

225 g (8 oz) onions, skinned
225 g (8 oz) green and gold peppers
397-g (14-oz) can Italian tomatoes
1 clove garlic, skinned
5 ml (1 tsp) oil (olive oil preferred)
225 g (8 oz) aubergines

2.5 ml ($\frac{1}{2}$ level tsp) salt
1.25 ml ($\frac{1}{4}$ level tsp) freshly ground
   pepper or good pinch powder
2.5 ml ($\frac{1}{2}$ level tsp) dried oregano
10 ml (2 tsp) wine vinegar

Slice the onions thinly. Halve the peppers lengthways and remove the core and seeds. Cut into long thin strips. Empty the tomatoes into a nylon strainer and leave to drain. Chop the garlic finely.

   Heat the oil in a wide heavy-based saucepan. Add the onions, cover the pan and cook for 5 minutes. Add the peppers, cover and continue cooking slowly for another 10 minutes. Meanwhile, prepare the aubergines. Peel them and cut into quarters lengthways. Lay the pieces on a board and cut across into 0.5-cm ($\frac{1}{4}$-in) slices. Stir the garlic into the softened onions and peppers. Mix in the aubergine and season with the salt, freshly ground pepper and oregano. Cover and simmer for 10 minutes, turning once. Add the tomatoes and vinegar, cover and cook gently for another 10 minutes. (The total cooking time is about 35 minutes.) Adjust the seasoning and serve very hot, or try serving cold.

   'Leanline' ratatouille makes a delicious starter and is excellent with hard-boiled eggs. It will store in the refrigerator, covered, for 2 days and freezes well too.

Serves 6

40 calories per serving

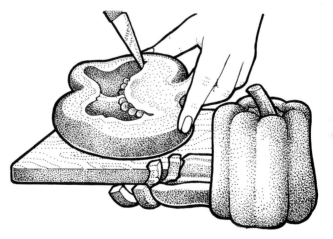

Cutting the core and seeds from a halved green pepper before slicing into long thin strips to make 'Leanline' ratatouille

Courgettes with leeks

Illustrated in colour on the jacket

450 g (1 lb) courgettes
225 g (8 oz) leeks
2.5 ml (½ level tsp) salt
6–8 twists of pepper from a mill or
   good pinch powder

1.25 ml (¼ level tsp) nutmeg, freshly
   grated if possible
150 ml (¼ pint) water
10 ml (2 tsp) lemon juice

Wash the courgettes, dry and cut off the ends. Do not peel but cut into 0.5-cm (¼-in) slices. Trim and wash the leeks. Cut away the coarse dark green part of the stalk. Cut right through the centre from top to bottom and chop into small dice; or slice the leeks. Wash in salted cold water. Drain and place in a wide heavy-based pan. Cover the leeks and cook over a low heat for 8–10 minutes. They will soften slightly and exude a certain amount of their own juice. Season with a little salt and pepper.

Add the courgettes and sprinkle lightly with salt, pepper and nutmeg. Pour in the water mixed with the lemon juice. Bring to the boil over a moderate heat, reduce the heat and cook gently for 5–8 minutes. Test after 5 minutes – the courgettes should be slightly crisp. Drain the vegetables and check the seasoning. This vegetable dish is equally good served cold.

Serves 4

30 calories per serving

Potatoes

The unadorned potato contains around 24 calories per 25 g (1 oz). Roasted, it creeps up to 35 calories and chipped it soars to 68 per 25 g (1 oz) (average thickness). New potatoes, boiled, reduce calories to 21 per 25 g (1 oz). So, provided you use no fat, the potato in small quantities becomes acceptable for inclusion in any healthy diet.

Boiled potatoes

The flavour of boiled new potatoes, correctly cooked, is delicious. A little fresh mint and parsley enhances the flavour and appearance. Choose potatoes of even size, scrub well but do not scrape or peel off the skin. Place in a saucepan, cover with boiling water and rapidly bring back to the boil. Add 7.5 ml (1½ level tsp) salt and a sprig of mint. Cover the pan and cook gently for 15 minutes until tender. Drain well and serve sprinkled with finely chopped parsley and a little more mint.

'Leanline' baked potato halves

Illustrated in colour facing page 76 and on the jacket

Old potatoes are decidedly better cooked in their skins. That is why baked potatoes are so full of flavour. Small ones are just as suitable for baking as large and take considerably less time to cook.

Scrub medium sized potatoes, about 175 g (6 oz) each, and cut them into two flat halves lengthways. Lightly score the surface and sprinkle it with salt. Place on a baking sheet and cook on the top shelf of the oven at 200°C (400°F) mark 6 for 35–45 minutes until the surface is crisp and the potato feels soft when gently squeezed. It is possible to bake these potatoes at a slightly lower or higher temperature, to fit in with cooking the meat etc, adjusting cooking times accordingly. For example, 190°C (375°F) mark 5 can be used when roasting chicken or lamb. Smaller or larger potatoes need a slight time adjustment. However, this method of potato cookery is so accommodating that it soon becomes popular with everyone who tries it. If you use the lower temperature of 180°C (350°F) mark 4 then it is advisable to brush the raw surface with oil. Serve with butter or plain yogurt mixed with chives.

175-g (6-oz) baked potato – 144 calories
plus 15 g ($\frac{1}{2}$ oz) butter – 113 calories
10 ml (2 tsp) natural yogurt – 10 calories

Spiced white cabbage

This aromatic cabbage blends well with chicken and, surprisingly, with fish, especially the richer varieties such as mackerel or herring. Of course, the cabbage must not be overcooked as it is always so much better when firm and slightly crisp.

700 g ($1\frac{1}{2}$ lb) firm white cabbage	2.5 ml ($\frac{1}{2}$ level tsp) salt
100 g (4 oz) onion, skinned	5-cm (2-in) strip orange peel
10 coriander seeds	150 ml ($\frac{1}{4}$ pint) cold water
6 whole black peppercorns	juice of 1 small orange
1 small clove garlic, skinned	15 ml (1 tbsp) natural yogurt
2.5 ml ($\frac{1}{2}$ level tsp) ground turmeric	

Remove any wilted outer leaves from the cabbage and divide into quarters. Cut away the thick stalk and slice finely. Wash thoroughly in lightly salted cold water and then drain in a colander. Slice the onion finely. Crush the coriander seeds, peppercorns and garlic with the turmeric and salt. Use a pestle and mortar or small basin and end of a rolling pin.

Layer half the cabbage and onion in a wide heavy-based saucepan or flameproof casserole. Add the orange peel and spicy paste. Cover with the remaining vegetables. Pour in the water and bring rapidly to the boil. Reduce the heat to low, add the orange juice and

simmer for 10 minutes. Stir and turn the cabbage once during cooking, so that it is coloured yellow by the turmeric. Check the seasoning – a little salt may be necessary. Stir in the yogurt and serve.
Serves 4

30 calories per serving

Lemony cabbage

Serve Lemony cabbage as a separate vegetable or use as a base for meat sauce or meat balls. It looks and tastes just as good as spaghetti or rice.

450–900 g (1–2 lb) white cabbage
1.1 litres (2 pints) water
5 ml (1 level tsp) salt

15 ml (1 tbsp) fresh or bottled lemon juice
freshly ground pepper

Divide the cabbage into quarters, removing the thick stalk, and slice the cabbage finely. Wash in plenty of cold water. Drain into a colander. Measure the water into a wide saucepan, bring to the boil and add the salt and lemon juice. Slide in the cabbage, partially cover and bring to the boil. Bubble over a moderate heat for 5 minutes only. Test with a fork – the cabbage should be crisp. Drain thoroughly and season with a little freshly ground pepper and a pinch of salt if necessary.

If liked, stir in one of the following: 15 ml (1 tbsp) yogurt; tiny strips of sweet red pepper; 5 ml (1 level tsp) finely grated lemon or orange peel.

15 calories per 100-g (4-oz)

'Leanline' red cabbage

Red cabbage is a sadly neglected vegetable. It is rich in vitamin C, especially raw. It is easy to prepare and cook and, unlike other vegetables, can be reheated. It is low in price as well as in calories so it is ideal for stretching a meal. This red cabbage recipe freezes well; remember to adjust the seasoning at the reheating stage.

900 g (2 lb) red cabbage
100 g (4 oz) onion, skinned
100 g (4 oz) carrot, peeled
2.5 ml ($\frac{1}{2}$ level tsp) salt
10 twists of pepper from a mill or
**   1.25 ml ($\frac{1}{4}$ level tsp) powder**

good pinch nutmeg
a strip of orange peel
1 bay leaf
30 ml (2 tbsp) wine or cider vinegar
60 ml (4 tbsp) water

Remove any wilted outer leaves. Divide the cabbage into quarters, cut away the thick stalk

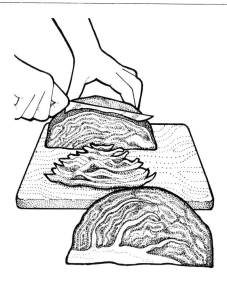

and slice the cabbage finely. Soak in cold salted water, using 5 ml (1 level tsp) salt, for 15 minutes. Drain into a colander.

Thinly slice the onion and carrot and place in a heavy-based saucepan or casserole. Add half the cabbage and season with a little salt, pepper and nutmeg. Bury the orange peel and bay leaf, cover with the rest of the cabbage and seasoning. Pour over the vinegar and water, cover the pan and cook over a gentle heat for 15 minutes until the contents are hot and bubbling. Keeping the heat low, simmer for 45 minutes on top of the cooker or in the centre of the oven at 150°C (300°F) mark 2. Check the seasoning before serving – the cabbage should be full flavoured and not over-salty.

If freezing the dish, cool with the lid off and then double wrap in foil. Reheat slowly, allowing at least 30 minutes from simmering point.
Serves 8

20 calories per 100-g (4-oz) serving

Wine-braised red cabbage

900 g (2 lb) red cabbage
25 g (1 oz) lean bacon
100 g (4 oz) carrot, peeled
100 g (4 oz) onion, skinned
1 stick celery with leaves
5 ml (1 level tsp) salt
10 twists of pepper from a mill or
   1.25 ml ($\frac{1}{4}$ level tsp) powder

1.25 ml ($\frac{1}{4}$ level tsp) nutmeg
1 bay leaf
1 clove
100 ml (4 fl oz) red wine
150 ml ($\frac{1}{4}$ pint) cold home made beef
   or chicken stock or make up using
   $\frac{1}{4}$ stock cube and leave to cool

Divide the cabbage into quarters and slice finely, removing the thick stalk. Rinse thoroughly in cold water and drain in a colander. Snip the bacon into tiny strips. Chop all the vegetables including the celery leaves. Layer all the ingredients into a large heavy-based saucepan or casserole, adding the seasonings, bay leaf and clove. Save a little seasoning for the final layer. Pour over the wine and cold stock.

Cover, place over a moderate heat and cook for about 15 minutes until the contents bubble before reducing the heat to low. Continue simmering for 45 minutes on top of the cooker or in the centre of the oven at 150°C (300°F) mark 2. If reheating this dish, allow at least 30 minutes from simmering point. *Note* Wine-braised red cabbage freezes well.
Serves 8

40 calories per serving

Jerusalem artichoke and carrot purée

Illustrated in colour facing page 77

450 g (1 lb) Jerusalem artichokes (see note)
10 ml (2 tsp) vinegar or lemon juice
225 g (8 oz) carrots, peeled
100 g (4 oz) onions, skinned
1.1 litres (2 pints) boiling water with 5 ml (1 level tsp) salt added
1 bay leaf

30–45 ml (2–3 tbsp) skimmed milk
pinch grated nutmeg
4–6 twists of pepper from a mill or good pinch powder
pinch salt
15 g (½ oz) butter
chopped fresh parsley to garnish

Wash and peel the artichokes, placing them in a bowl of cold water containing the vinegar or lemon juice. Halve or quarter them so that they are about the same size. Cut the carrots into small chunks. Thinly slice the onion. Drain the artichokes and slide them into the boiling salted water. Add the carrot, onion and bay leaf.

Partially cover the pan and boil for 10–15 minutes, until the vegetables are tender but firm when pricked with a fork. Drain thoroughly, tip into a bowl and mash to a purée working in the skimmed milk, nutmeg, pepper and salt to taste. Stir in the butter. If you purée the vegetables in an electric blender, do not add more than 45 ml (3 tbsp) skimmed milk or the final purée will be too wet.

Reheat over a moderate heat, uncovered, stirring from time to time, or in the centre of the oven at 190°C (375°F) mark 5 for 15–20 minutes until hot.
Note Jerusalem artichokes have a sweet delicate flavour. Raw Jerusalem artichokes should be firm and not spongy. They may be scrubbed and cooked with the peel on. Serve them whole or cut into thick slices.
Serves 4

65 calories per serving

Leek and swede purée

Illustrated in colour facing page 76

450 g (1 lb) leeks
5 ml (1 level tsp) salt
8–10 twists of pepper from a mill or
 1.25 ml ($\frac{1}{4}$ level tsp) powder
350 g (12 oz) swedes
cold water to cover
1 bay leaf

30–45 ml (2–3 tbsp) hot cooking liquid
5 ml (1 level tsp) grated raw
 horseradish or 10 ml (2 level tsp)
 horseradish relish or sauce
1.25 ml ($\frac{1}{4}$ level tsp) grated nutmeg
15 g ($\frac{1}{2}$ oz) butter (optional)
chopped fresh parsley to garnish

Cut away the coarse dark green part of the leek stalks. Slice finely, wash thoroughly in plenty of cold water and leave to soak for 10 minutes in lightly salted cold water. Drain and put them into a wide heavy-based or non-stick pan. Cover and sweat them over a low heat for 8–10 minutes. The leeks will soften and exude some of their juices. Sprinkle with a little salt and pepper.

Peel, wash and dry the swedes. Cut into small chunks. Spread them over the leeks and season lightly with salt and pepper. Cover with cold water. Add the bay leaf and 5 ml (1 level tsp) salt. Rapidly bring to the boil, reduce the heat to medium and cook for 10 minutes. The vegetables should be just tender.

Reserving a little of the hot liquid to add to the purée, drain the vegetables into a colander. Remove the bay leaf. Purée in a blender or mouli-legumes, or use a potato masher. There may be small pieces of leek incorporated in the final purée but this is preferable to sieving them. Stir in the horseradish, nutmeg and a little salt and pepper. If liked, add 15 g ($\frac{1}{2}$ oz) butter to the purée; add a very little of the hot cooking liquid only if necessary. If using a blender do not add too much liquid; the final purée should be on the dry side.

Reheat uncovered over a low heat on top of the cooker or in the oven at 180°C (350°F) mark 4 for 15–20 minutes until very hot.

For an interesting snack, serve with poached eggs (see following recipe).

Serves 4

---

45 calories per serving
70 calories per serving with butter added

Poached eggs

Try poached eggs on a bed of Leek and swede purée. Or serve with a small 100-g (4-oz) baked potato and you have a substantial satisfying meal.

It is a pity so many people insist on using specially designed egg poachers, which often produce leathery eggs with oily butter, quite different from the classic poached egg. Since egg yolk contains 32 per cent fat, eggs poached in water do not need butter.

A little practice will soon convince you that real poached eggs are actually less troublesome to prepare than those cooked in an egg poacher. Ideally, the eggs should be at room temperature and two or three days old as the white of a really new laid egg (rarely obtainable nowadays) will not hold its shape. Refrigerated eggs will be too cold. Stale eggs are unsuitable for poaching as their yolks tend to break easily. Do not poach more than two eggs at a time. It is better to perfect your technique with one before attempting two!

Use a medium size 15–18-cm (6–7-in) frying pan. Pour in boiling water to a depth of 2.5 cm (1 in), so that it is three quarters full. Add 10 ml (2 tsp) wine or cider vinegar, which speeds up coagulation. Unless you love the flavour of malt vinegar, avoid it, as its all pervasive smell will be absorbed by the egg.

Bring the water to a gentle simmer. Break each egg separately into a cup. Hold the cup low over the water and slide in the egg. Repeat immediately with the second egg. Poach for 3 minutes, using a timer. Lift them out with a long-handled perforated spoon and serve very hot.

---

1 egg, size 2 – 90 calories

plus a serving of leek and swede purée – 45 calories

100-g (4-oz) jacket potato – 90 calories

Carrots in chicken stock

Cooking with real chicken stock makes a tremendous difference to this dish, as well as to many other vegetables.

450 g (1 lb) carrots, peeled
150 ml ($\frac{1}{4}$ pint) home made chicken stock or make up using $\frac{1}{4}$ chicken stock cube
1.25 ml ($\frac{1}{4}$ level tsp) salt or to taste

5–6 twists of pepper from a mill or good pinch powder
5 ml (1 tsp) finely chopped fresh parsley

Use a mouli-julienne (disc no. 4) or coarsely grate or chop the carrots. Put them in a wide heavy-based saucepan and pour in the cold stock. Cover the pan and bring to the boil over a moderate heat. Cook for 5 minutes, uncover, raise the heat and boil hard for 3 minutes until the stock is reduced to about 15–30 ml (1–2 tbsp) and the carrots are shiny. Season with salt and pepper and sprinkle with the chopped parsley.

Note It is important not to add the seasoning until the cooking is complete. If using stock made with a cube this will add a certain amount of salt to the carrots.

Serves 4

25 calories per serving

Salad platter

A display of crisp, colourful vegetables is always attractive. Raw fennel with beetroot is particularly pleasing to eye and palate.

lettuce leaves
watercress sprigs
1 350-g (12-oz) fennel bulb
lemon juice
about 225 g (8 oz) cooked beetroot
3 spring onions
little finely chopped mint

For the yogurt mint dressing
141-g (5-oz) carton natural yogurt
5 ml (1 tsp) lemon juice
salt and freshly ground pepper
$\frac{1}{2}$ clove of garlic, skinned and crushed
2.5 ml ($\frac{1}{2}$ tsp) finely chopped mint

Remove wilted leaves and the coarse stalks of green salad vegetables and wash in plenty of cold water. Drain and dry them as thoroughly as possible, preferably in one of the salad drainers now available. Store in the refrigerator in a dry tea towel or polythene bag.

Cut the leafy tops off the fennel. Do not discard them as they add interest and flavour to many fish dishes. (Fennel trimmings keep fresh for up to a week stored in a polythene bag in the refrigerator.) Remove any bruised or wilted parts of the bulb. Slice off about 0.3 cm ($\frac{1}{8}$ in) from the base. Halve, wash in cold water then dry thoroughly. Grate the fennel coarsely, if possible with the mouli-julienne, or slice it very thinly. Sprinkle with a little lemon juice. Peel and cut the beetroot into small cubes. Clean the spring onions and chop finely. Pile the fennel into the centre of a platter. Surround with the cubed beetroot and then with the washed and torn lettuce leaves and sprigs of watercress. Sprinkle the mint and spring onions over the fennel and beetroot.

Stir the dressing ingredients together and pour over the salad just before serving.

Serves 6

35 calories per serving (including dressing)
(75 calories for the dressing)

Colourful winter salad

An ideal standby for hungry slimmers as large helpings equal few calories! There are so many good nourishing vegetables available in the winter months which beg to be eaten raw. Be adventurous with combinations of vegetables and try adding a little fruit just

Apricot cheesecake (page 105),
Tangy fruit jelly (page 101), ▶
'Leanline' confectioner's custard (page 106)

before serving. Seedless tangerines or segments of orange go particularly well with red cabbage. One fruit will add approximately 50 calories to the total.

225 g (8 oz) red cabbage
100 g (4 oz) carrot, peeled
50 g (2 oz) onion, skinned
100 g (4 oz) Brussels sprouts, washed
  and trimmed
100 g (4 oz) crisp apple
30 ml (2 tbsp) lemon juice

For the orange yogurt salad dressing
141-g (5-oz) carton natural yogurt
5 ml (1 tsp) grated orange peel
pinch nutmeg
salt and freshly ground pepper

Use the coarse blade of a mouli-julienne or a grater to obtain a crunchy mixture. Leave the peel on the apple, remove the core and cut into quarters then into small chunks. Tip all the ingredients into a large bowl and sprinkle over the lemon juice. For the dressing, stir all the ingredients together. Add the salad to the dressing, mixing well to coat evenly.

This salad, without dressing, may be stored, covered, in the refrigerator for 3 days. *Serves 6–8*

40 calories per serving including dressing (for six)
30 calories per serving including dressing (for eight)
(75 calories for the dressing)

Reviving winter crunchy salad

Illustrated in colour facing page 77

This salad is rich in vitamins and is very welcome during the over indulgent Christmas and New Year period. It does wonders for flagging digestion. Serve it with cold turkey on Boxing Day when it will receive the attention it deserves.

350 g (12 oz) white cabbage
225 g (8 oz) carrots, peeled
1 small onion, skinned
50 g (2 oz) red pepper
1 satsuma
15 g ($\frac{1}{2}$ oz) currants
5 ml (1 level tsp) finely grated orange
  rind

For the orange and mint salad dressing
141-g (5-oz) carton natural yogurt
5 ml (1 level tsp) grated orange peel
15 ml (1 tbsp) orange juice
2.5 ml ($\frac{1}{2}$ level tsp) dried mint
6 twists of pepper from a mill or
  pinch powder
1.25 ml ($\frac{1}{4}$ level tsp) salt

Wash the cabbage and dry thoroughly. Using a mouli-julienne (disc no. 4) or the coarse side of a grater, grate or shred the cabbage, carrots and onion into a large bowl. Wash and deseed the pepper. Cut away the stalk and core and ensure that every seed is removed. Dry on kitchen paper towel and cut into long thin strips. Peel the satsuma and strip away all the pith. Slice and mix into the salad together with the currants and orange rind.

'Leanline' fatless sponge with summer fruit filling
◀ *(page 108), Lean date and cherry fruit cake (page 111),*
'Leanline' sticky fruit cake (page 113)

For the dressing, stir all the ingredients together and pour over the salad. Scatter with the red pepper strips. The dressing may be stored, covered, in the refrigerator for 2 days. *Serves 6*

45 calories per serving (including dressing)
(80 calories for the dressing)

Brown rice

Illustrated in colour facing page 45

When I first decided to cook brown rice I thumbed my way through literally dozens of cookbooks for explicit instructions. Vague suggestions of 'cook until soft' or 'it takes longer to cook than white' did not help. By trial and error I found that brown rice is easier to cook than white and more adaptable than I had been led to expect.

The secret is to pre-soak the rice in cold water – for several hours if possible, but a couple of hours will do. After soaking, drain into a nylon strainer and rinse under running cold water.

Brown rice does not swell as much as white so allow 50 g (2 oz) raw long grain brown rice per serving. *225 g (8 oz) will give four generous helpings.*

Place 225 g (8 oz) soaked, washed and drained brown rice in a saucepan. Add 600 ml (1 pint) cold water and 5 ml (1 level tsp) salt and (optional but pleasant) 10 ml (2 tsp) lemon juice. Cover and bring to the boil over a moderate heat. Lower the heat so that the water is maintained at a gentle simmer; partially cover with a lid and cook for 30 minutes. Check from time to time to make sure that the rice is cooked gently so that the water is gradually absorbed. If it cooks too quickly the rice will soak up the water but remain uncooked. I find that 30 minutes is about right for pre-soaked long grain rice by which time it absorbs all the water and results in a good chewy, nutty texture. Extra seasoning may be added just before serving. Too much salt in the cooking liquid will result in over-salty rice.

Try cooking in real chicken stock for a specially good flavour. Brown rice may be kept hot in the oven at 150°C (300°F) mark 2 with a little liquid – stock for preference but water will do – and covered with foil. It reheats well too with a very small quantity of water or stock, about 150 ml ($\frac{1}{4}$ pint), over a medium heat, covered. Turn the rice over during the reheating period.

Serving suggestion
Beansprouts, drained and rinsed under running cold water, blend particularly well with brown rice and stretch the calories. Mix them with the hot rice for the last 3 minutes, tossing to absorb the heat. 5 ml (1 tsp) soy sauce stirred in just before serving enhances the final flavour.

50 g (2 oz) boiled brown rice – 70 calories
25 g (1 oz) beansprouts – 8 calories

Puddings and desserts

Anyone trying to lose weight must relinquish conventional calorie laden puddings. Instead of these, I have created a range of light and temptingly delicious 'Leanline' desserts.

The intractable problem of sweetening has been solved by using fruit sugar (fructose) (see Sweetening agents, page 16) and, wherever possible, the natural flavours of fruit. I have included three cheesecakes in this section which show various fillings and methods of sweetening, as well as crushed crumb bases. I believe these recipes will convince you that a satisfying end to a pleasurable meal is always possible.

Apple and date meringue

450 g (1 lb) cooking apples
25 g (1 oz) dates
45 ml (3 tbsp) water
10 ml (2 tsp) lemon juice

2 large egg whites, at room
temperature
25 g (1 oz) caster sugar

Peel, core and thinly slice the apples into a bowl of water with a squeeze of lemon juice added. Chop the dates as finely as possible. Drain the apples into a colander. Put the water and lemon juice into a wide heavy-based saucepan. Add a layer of apples, then dates, and finish with a covering of apples. Cover the pan and place over a moderate heat. Cook for 15 minutes until the apples are soft, turning once and reducing the heat if necessary. Uncover the pan and let the fruit bubble for a few minutes to evaporate some of the liquid. The mixture should be thick. A little artificial sweetener may be added at this stage although the dates should give sufficient sweetness. Turn the apple and date mixture into an ovenproof 900-ml (1½-pint) pie dish or similar size dish. Place in the centre of the oven at 180°C (350°F) mark 4 to keep hot.

Put the egg whites into a large dry bowl. Whisk until foamy, then sift in half the sugar. Continue to whisk until the whites are glossy and stiff. Lightly fold in the remaining sugar. Spoon the meringue over the hot fruit purée. Return to the oven for 10 minutes to brown and crisp the meringue.

Note If you cook the fruit purée in advance, heat in the oven (same temperature as above) for 20–30 minutes, depending on the depth of the dish used and the coldness of the fruit. Then top with meringue.

Serves 4

85 calories per serving

Orange baked bananas with apricots

100 g (4 oz) dried apricots
strip of orange peel
1 vanilla pod

4 150-g (5-oz) bananas, weighed with
 skin
juice of 1 orange

Wash the apricots. Cover with cold water and soak overnight or for several hours. Tip the apricots and water into a saucepan; add the strip of orange peel and the vanilla pod snipped in three pieces. Bring up to the boil over a moderate heat and simmer for 10 minutes. Remove and cool, leaving the pod and peel in the syrup.

Place the apricots in a single layer over the base of an ovenproof dish. Peel the bananas and lay them on top. Squeeze the orange, mix with sufficient apricot syrup to make 150 ml ($\frac{1}{4}$ pint) and pour over the fruit. Cover the dish with foil and cook in the oven, one shelf above centre, at 180°C (350°F) mark 4 for 35 minutes. Serve with the hot syrup and single cream.

Note Do not substitute vanilla essence for the pod. The true vanilla flavour perfumes the apricots and syrup. After use, wash the pieces of vanilla pod in warm water, *dry thoroughly* and store in an airtight container.
Serves 4

90 calories per serving
plus 50 ml (2 tbsp) single cream – 62 calories

Apple, apricot and prune party pudding

150 ml ($\frac{1}{4}$ pint) dry red wine
12 large prunes, about 100 g (4 oz)
100 g (4 oz) whole dried apricots
strip of orange peel
juice of 1 orange
$\frac{1}{3}$ vanilla pod or 2.5 ml ($\frac{1}{2}$ tsp) vanilla
 essence

900 g (2 lb) cooking apples
30 ml (2 tbsp) water
10 ml (2 tsp) lemon juice
15 g ($\frac{1}{2}$ oz) toasted flaked almonds

All the fruits may be prepared a day in advance. Cool, cover and store in the refrigerator. Assemble several hours before serving so that the flavours mellow.

Pour the wine over the prunes and leave to soak overnight. Partially cover and simmer for 5 minutes. The prunes will absorb most of the wine. Drain over a bowl and keep the wine syrup. Slit the prunes and carefully remove the stones, using a small sharp knife.

Wash the apricots, drain and place them in a bowl. Pare away a strip of orange peel, squeeze out the juice and pour over the apricots. Add sufficient cold water to barely cover the fruit. Soak for at least 2 hours or overnight.

Tip the apricots and orange-flavoured water into a medium size pan; add the strip of orange peel and piece of vanilla pod or essence. Cover the pan and bring slowly to the boil. Cook gently for 5 minutes. The apricots should be slightly undercooked. Pour into a bowl to cool. Leave the apricots in the juice until needed for the final decoration.

Peel, core and slice the apples into a bowl of cold water. Drain. Put them into a wide saucepan with the 30 ml (2 tbsp) water and sprinkle them with lemon juice. Cover the pan and cook over a moderate heat. After 5 minutes, turn them over and continue cooking until they are pulpy – about 15 minutes. Pour into a nylon strainer to remove surplus liquid. Tip the apple into a bowl and stir in the red wine syrup. Add 15–30 ml (1–2 tbsp) of the apricot syrup. No other sweetening is necessary. The purée should be well flavoured by the two syrups.

Spread the apple purée over the base of a wide shallow dish. Drain the apricots. Lay them on the purée, alternating with the prunes, giving a criss-cross effect. Decorate with the toasted flaked almonds. Serve with single cream. For a special treat, serve with small meringues or fingers of fatless sponge as these are lighter than shortbread or almond biscuits.

Serves 10

---

65 calories per serving
plus 50 ml (2 tbsp) single cream – 60 calories

Lean apple purée

450 g (1 lb) cooking apples, Bramleys preferably
15 ml (1 tbsp) water
2.5 ml (½ level tsp) cinnamon or ⅓ cinnamon stick
1 clove
5 ml (1 level tsp) black treacle
2–3 drops liquid artificial sweetener

Peel, core and slice the apples into a bowl of cold water. Drain and put them into a saucepan with the water, cinnamon and clove. Cook over a moderate heat with the lid on. Turn them over after 5 minutes and continue cooking until the apples are pulpy – about 15 minutes in all.

Pour away most of the liquid, stir in the treacle and taste, adding liquid artificial sweetener as required. Purée in a blender or mash well with a fork. Cool. This can be stored, covered, for up to 5 days in the refrigerator.

Note Double the quantity may be made so that you have a supply available. Use 30 ml (2 tbsp) water for 900 g (2 lb) apples but do not increase the spices. Try mixing Lean apple purée with a fruit yogurt for a quick dessert – blackcurrant goes particularly well. (But remember to add on the extra calories!)

Serves 4

---

50 calories per serving

Blackberry and port mousse

Port and blackberries combine particularly well. However, blackberry mousse is also enjoyable without alcohol.

450 g (1 lb) fresh or frozen
  blackberries
15 g (½ oz) fruit sugar
30 ml (2 tbsp) cold water
little artificial sweetener

15-g (½-oz) packet gelatine
60 ml (4 tbsp) cold water
15 ml (1 tbsp) lemon juice
141-g (5-oz) carton natural yogurt
30 ml (2 tbsp) port

Put the blackberries, fruit sugar and cold water in a saucepan. Place over a low heat, cover and simmer for 10 minutes, until the fruit is tender. Add a little artificial sweetener to the hot liquid and leave to cool. Sprinkle the gelatine into the 60 ml (4 tbsp) cold water. Soak for a few minutes and then dissolve over a low heat, stirring all the time. Do not boil.

Purée the cooled blackberries with 150 ml (¼ pint) of the cooking juices, lemon juice and yogurt. Stir in the gelatine and finally the port. Alternatively sieve the fruit then gradually work in all the other ingredients. Cover and chill in the refrigerator.

Serves 6

60 calories per serving
50 calories per serving (without port)

Minted gooseberry mousse

This pretty pale green mousse is a refreshing dessert and adds an interesting touch to a summer buffet or dinner.

450 g (1 lb) gooseberries
15 ml (1 tbsp) scissor-snipped mint
  leaves
30 ml (2 tbsp) water
25 g (1 oz) fruit sugar
2–3 tablets artificial sweetener
15 ml (1 tbsp) lemon juice

60 ml (4 tbsp) cold water
15-ml (½-oz) packet gelatine
141-g (5-oz) carton natural yogurt
2–3 drops green food colouring
2 egg whites, at room temperature
15 g (½ oz) caster sugar

Top and tail the gooseberries. Put them in a wide heavy-based saucepan with the mint leaves, water and fruit sugar. Cover, place over low heat and cook gently for 15 minutes or until the fruit is tender. Drain off about half the liquid and reserve. To dissolve the sweetener, add it to the hot fruit. Purée the fruit in a blender or mouli food mill – there should be 450 ml (¾ pint). If necessary, add a little of the reserved gooseberry juice. Add the lemon juice.

Measure the 60 ml (4 tbsp) cold water into a small saucepan. Sprinkle in the gelatine, leave to soak for a few minutes and then dissolve over very low heat, stirring all the time. Cool slightly and blend it into the purée. Pour the cooled purée into a large bowl and stir in the yogurt and green food colouring.

In a large dry bowl, whisk the egg whites until they are foamy and stand in soft peaks. Sift in the caster sugar and whisk continuously until glossy and stiff. Fold quickly and lightly into the purée. Spoon into individual glass dishes or a medium size soufflé dish. Cover loosely with foil and chill in the refrigerator.

Serves 6

60 calories per serving

'Leanline' lemon mousse

100 ml (4 fl oz) cold water
15-g (½-oz) packet gelatine
4 eggs, size 2 (at room temperature)
25 g (1 oz) fruit sugar

finely grated rind of 1 lemon
juice of 2 lemons, about 60–75 ml
  (4–5 tbsp)
25 g (1 oz) caster sugar

Measure the water into a small saucepan, sprinkle in the gelatine and leave to soak. Separate the eggs. Pour the whites into a large clean bowl. Put the yolks, fruit sugar and grated lemon rind into a mixing bowl. Work together with a rotary beater or wooden spoon and stir in the lemon juice.

Dissolve the gelatine over a low heat. Do not boil. Remove and allow to cool slightly before whisking into the lemon mixture. Leave to become cold and slightly thickened. Whisk the egg whites to a foam. Sprinkle with the caster sugar and continue to whisk until shiny and firm. Fold quickly and lightly into the lemon mixture. Pour into a large soufflé dish or individual dishes.

Chill in a cool place or in the bottom of the refrigerator. When set, loosely cover with foil to prevent the surface becoming dry.

Serves 8

80 calories per serving

Raspberry whip

Illustrated in colour on the jacket

60 ml (4 tbsp) cold water
15-g (½-oz) packet gelatine
350 g (12 oz) fresh or frozen
  raspberries
15 g (½ oz) fruit sugar

finely grated rind and juice of
  1 orange
141-g (5-oz) carton natural yogurt
2 egg whites, at room temperature
15 g (½ oz) caster sugar

Measure the cold water into a small saucepan and sprinkle in the gelatine. Leave to soak. Frozen raspberries should be thawed and the juice added for blending. Purée the fruit in a blender with the fruit sugar, orange rind and juice and any juice from the raspberries. Dissolve the gelatine over a low heat. Cool and blend into the fruit purée. Turn into a large bowl and stir in the yogurt. The purée should be completely cold.

In a large dry bowl, whisk the egg whites until they are foamy and stand in soft peaks. Sift in the caster sugar and whisk continuously until glossy and stiff. Fold into the raspberry purée. Spoon into individual glass dishes or a medium size soufflé dish. Cover loosely with foil and leave to set in a cool place or on the lowest shelf in the refrigerator.
Serves 6

50 calories per serving

Tangy fruit jelly

Illustrated in colour facing page 92

150 ml ($\frac{1}{4}$ pint) cold water
15-g ($\frac{1}{2}$-oz) packet gelatine
1 grapefruit
$\frac{1}{2}$ sweet melon, weighing about 550 g
   (1 lb 4 oz) with skin
5 ml (1 level tsp) fruit sugar

juice of 1 small orange, about 50 ml
   (2 tbsp)
2 tablets artificial sweetener or liquid
   sweetener to taste
24-ml (8.5-fl oz) bottle low-calorie
   bitter lemon, well chilled

Measure the cold water into a small saucepan. Sprinkle in the gelatine and leave to soak. Remove all the peel and pith from the grapefruit by holding the fruit over a bowl and, starting at the top, sawing through peel and pith with a serrated-edged knife. Cut the fruit into small pieces, lifting away membrane and pips. Strain the grapefruit juice into a measuring jug. Place the grapefruit pieces in a suitable serving bowl or mould.

Scrape out the melon seeds. Holding the melon over the bowl to catch the juices, remove the flesh with a vegetable scoop or teaspoon. Squeeze the melon shell to extract all the juice. Add the melon juice to the jug. Mix the melon balls with the grapefruit pieces. Sprinkle with the fruit sugar.

Squeeze the orange and add the strained juice to the mixed fruit juices. Dissolve the gelatine over a low heat. Do not boil. Turn off heat and add the artificial sweetener. Stir until dissolved in the hot gelatine. Cool and stir into the fruit juices. Allow to cool completely before adding the well chilled bitter lemon. The total liquid should be just under 600 ml (1 pint). Make up with iced water if necessary. Mix into the fruit and place in the refrigerator. When set, cover with foil. Turn the jelly out and serve with extra melon and grapefruit.
Serves 6

30 calories per serving

Rhubarb and orange fool

700 g (1½ lb) rhubarb
15 ml (1 tbsp) cold water
5 ml (1 level tsp) grated orange rind
5 ml (1 level tsp) black treacle
little artificial sweetener or 25 g (1 oz)
   demerara sugar

1 orange
60 ml (4 tbsp) cold water
15-g (½-oz) packet gelatine
141-g (5-oz) carton natural yogurt
thin orange slices to decorate

Wash and trim the rhubarb and cut into short lengths. Place in a wide shallow saucepan. Sprinkle with the water and grated orange rind. Cover the pan and cook over low heat for 15 minutes until the fruit is soft. Drain away most of the water. Stir in the treacle and the artificial sweetener or demerara sugar. Keep the artificial sweetener to a minimum – about 2–3 tablets.

Tip the drained and sweetened rhubarb into a blender. Add the orange flesh – pith and pips removed. Blend to a purée. If you do not have a blender, use a fork. Measure the 60 ml (4 tbsp) cold water into a small saucepan, sprinkle in the gelatine and soak for a few minutes. Dissolve the gelatine over a very low heat, stirring. Do not boil. Cool slightly and blend into the rhubarb purée. When the mixture is quite cold, gently fold in the yogurt.

This rosy and white fool looks pretty set in small glass dishes. Chill in the refrigerator loosely covered with foil. Decorate with thin orange slices when the mousse has set.
Serves 6

65 calories per serving (using demerara sugar)
45 calories per serving (using artificial sweetener)

Rhubarb meringue

700 g (1½ lb) rhubarb
boiling water to cover
5 ml (1 level tsp) grated orange rind
30 ml (2 tbsp) orange juice or juice of
   1 small orange

2 175-g (6-oz) ripe bananas, weighed
   with skin
2 large egg whites, at room
   temperature
15 g (½ oz) caster sugar

Trim the rhubarb, cut into short lengths and wash in cold water. Drain, place in a large saucepan and cover with boiling water. Leave for 5 minutes and drain into a colander. (This short immersion in boiling water considerably reduces the oxalic acid content of rhubarb. It then becomes acceptable to many people who find the acidity objectionable.) Tip the rhubarb into a shallow heavy-based pan, add 15 ml (1 tbsp) water, cover and simmer for 5–10 minutes until soft. Stir in the orange rind and juice. Set aside to cool and absorb the orange flavour. When quite cold, drain off surplus liquid and purée with the bananas in a blender.

For the meringue, whisk the egg whites in a large dry bowl until they are foamy and stand in soft peaks. Sift in the caster sugar and whisk continuously until the mixture is smooth, glossy and firm. Using a plastic spatula, fold the meringue, lightly and quickly, into the fruit. Do not overwork the mixture at this stage. A few white streaks give a pretty marbling effect. Spoon into 6 individual glass dishes. Cover loosely with foil. Chill for 1 hour before serving.
Serves 6

65 calories per serving

Luxury lemon cheesecake

For the base
6 Rich Tea biscuits
1.25 ml ($\frac{1}{4}$ level tsp) cinnamon
1.25 ml ($\frac{1}{4}$ level tsp) ground nutmeg
25 g (1 oz) low fat spread

For the filling
30 ml (2 tbsp) cold water
15-g ($\frac{1}{2}$-oz) packet gelatine
3 eggs, separated

225 g (8 oz) cottage cheese
225 g (8 oz) medium fat curd cheese
15 g ($\frac{1}{2}$ oz) caster sugar
grated rind and juice of 1 large lemon
141-g (5-oz) carton soured cream
few drops of liquid artificial
  sweetener
25 g (1 oz) dried apricots, washed,
  dried and cut into strips

Place the biscuits in a polythene bag and crush them using a rolling pin. Shake the spices into the crumbs in the bag. Melt the fat over a low heat. Add the crumbs and stir until coated. Spoon into a shallow dish about 20.5 cm (8 in) wide and not more than 5 cm (2 in) deep (see *Note*.)

Put the cold water into a small saucepan, sprinkle over the gelatine and leave to soak. Beat together the yolks, cottage and curd cheeses, sugar, lemon rind and soured cream until blended. Work in the lemon juice and add a little artificial sweetener to taste – try not to oversweeten as it tends to destroy the lovely flavours.

Melt the gelatine over a low heat; do not boil. Stir until dissolved. Cool and beat into the lemon mixture. Whip the egg whites until stiff. Fold into the lemon mixture together with the apricots. Pour on to the crumb base and set in the refrigerator, covered with foil.

Note A fluted 23-cm (9-in) china flan dish means you don't have to turn the cake out. Another useful tip is to use a large lightly greased flan ring on a flat plate, spoon in the crumbs and pour on the cheesecake mixture. Lift off the ring when the cake has set and is ready to serve.

This cheesecake freezes well.

Serves 10

160 calories per serving

Lean lemon cheesecake

For the base
5 French toasts or Dutch rusks
25 g (1 oz) low fat spread
1.25 ml ($\frac{1}{4}$ level tsp) cinnamon
1.25 ml ($\frac{1}{4}$ level tsp) ginger

For the filling
60 ml (4 tbsp) cold water

15-g ($\frac{1}{2}$-oz) packet gelatine
2 eggs, size 3
grated rind and juice of 1 lemon
225 g (8 oz) cottage cheese
141-g (5-oz) carton natural yogurt
15 g ($\frac{1}{2}$ oz) fruit sugar
2–3 drops liquid artificial sweetener
15 g ($\frac{1}{2}$ oz) sultanas

Crush the toasts or rusks to a fine crumb by placing them in a polythene bag and crushing with a rolling pin. Melt the fat over a low heat and stir in the crumbs and spices. Spoon this mixture into a shallow dish. A 20.5-cm (8-in) white china flan dish looks most attractive, or use a lightly oiled flan ring on a flat dinner plate. (See Luxury lemon cheesecake note.)

Measure the cold water into a small saucepan, sprinkle in the gelatine and leave to soak. Separate the eggs, using a large bowl for the whites. Cream together the yolks, lemon rind and juice, cottage cheese, yogurt, fruit sugar and artificial sweetener; or use a blender which will give a smoother mixture. Melt the gelatine over a low heat. Do not allow to boil. Stir until dissolved and then remove from the heat. Cool slightly before adding to the lemon mixture either by setting the blender speed to low and pouring the gelatine through the hole in the lid or by using an electric beater or wooden spoon to work in the gelatine.

Add the sultanas. Whip the egg whites until stiff, then lightly and quickly fold them into the cheesecake mixture. Pour on to the crumb base and refrigerate or leave in a cold larder to set. Cover with foil.

Note Curd cheese, although slightly higher in calories than cottage cheese, is an excellent alternative if you have to hand-mix the cheesecake. It is smooth and creams easily.

This cheesecake freezes well.

Serves 8

115 calories per serving

Apricot cheesecake

Illustrated in colour facing page 92

50 g (2 oz) plain biscuits (Petit beurre or Nice), crushed
60 ml (4 tbsp) cold water
15-g (½-oz) packet gelatine
225 g (8 oz) curd cheese
2 eggs, separated
141-g (5-oz) carton natural yogurt

grated rind and juice of 1 lemon
15 g (½ oz) fruit sugar
15 g (½ oz) caster sugar
a little artificial sweetener to taste
50 g (2 oz) cooked dried apricots, well drained

A 20.5-cm (8-in) shallow china or glass flan dish eliminates the problem of turning out the finished cake. Alternatively, place a lightly oiled 20.5-cm (8-in) flan ring on a flat dinner plate and simply lift the ring off when the cake has set.

Put the biscuits in a polythene bag and crush them with a rolling pin. Spread the crushed biscuit over the bottom of the dish or plate. Measure the water into a small saucepan, sprinkle in the gelatine and leave to soak. In a large bowl, cream together the curd cheese, egg yolks, yogurt, grated lemon rind, fruit sugar and caster sugar. Gradually work in the lemon juice.

Dissolve the gelatine over a very low heat, stirring continuously. Do not allow to boil. Remove from the heat and cool slightly before blending into the cheese mixture. Whisk thoroughly with an electric or rotary whisk for a minute or so, to achieve a smooth texture. A little artificial sweetener may be added at this point. Scissor-snip the apricots and stir them into the cheese mixture. Whip the egg whites until stiff and fold lightly and quickly into the cooled mixture. Turn into the flan dish and leave to set in a cold larder or on the lowest shelf in the refrigerator. Cover loosely with foil. Remove from the refrigerator an hour before serving. If liked, this can be decorated with well drained canned apricot halves.

Serves 8

110 calories per serving
25 g (1 oz) drained canned apricots – 30 calories

'Leanline' confectioner's custard

Illustrated in colour facing page 92

1 vanilla pod
450 ml ($\frac{3}{4}$ pint) skimmed milk
2 egg yolks
1 egg, size 3

15 g ($\frac{1}{2}$ oz) caster sugar
15 g ($\frac{1}{2}$ oz) fruit sugar
15 g ($\frac{1}{2}$ oz) plain flour

Cut the vanilla pod into 3 pieces and add to the milk in a heavy-based small saucepan. Leave aside for the milk to absorb the vanilla flavour. Break the yolks and the whole egg into a medium size bowl. Add the sugars and sift in the flour. Using an electric beater or whisk, beat the egg mixture for a few minutes until it is smooth and creamy.

Place the vanilla-flavoured milk over a low heat and bring it to just below boiling point. Remove the vanilla pod. Gradually whisk the hot milk into the egg mixture. Pour this thin custard into the saucepan. Add the vanilla pod. Place over a very low heat and stir continuously for 5–10 minutes until the custard thickens sufficiently to coat the back of a wooden spoon.

Strain the custard into a clean bowl. Soak a circle of greaseproof paper in cold water, squeeze to remove surplus moisture and lay it on the surface of the custard. Allow to cool. Cover the bowl with foil and store in the refrigerator. This method of covering keeps the custard fresh for 3 days.

Wash the pieces of vanilla pod in warm water. Dry them thoroughly and store in a screw-topped jar.

Serve this custard with fresh or cooked fruit, or blend it with natural yogurt for a creamy dessert. 15 ml (1 tbsp) orange-based liqueur (about 50 calories), stirred into the cold custard, transforms it into dinner party fare. Also luscious served with strawberries! Another way to sweeten is to stir in 5 ml (1 tsp) clear honey (40 calories) and the minimum of artificial sweetener.

---

545 calories for the confectioner's custard

Cakes and bread

During the early days of 'Leanline' classes I was constantly made aware that giving up cake was intolerable. Weekend family tea increased the weight and, consequently, lowered the morale of many of my students.

Creating a 'Leanline' cake was indeed a challenging proposition as my aim was a real fruit cake, and not a synthetic substitute. Eventually, 'Leanline' sticky fruit cake fulfilled this ambition. It was so well received that a banana based cake soon followed. Both these cakes contain All-Bran and are fatless. Nevertheless, they are moist and store well, wrapped in foil.

Two delicious, more conventional, fruit cakes are included. They demonstrate how to use low fat spread as well as fruit sugar. The dried fruits used are chosen for maximum flavour and sweetness.

The weight of these cakes may vary a little, but they contain approximately half the calories of the usual fruit cake.

The 'Leanline' fatless sponge

Illustrated in colour facing page 93

A feather-light whisked sponge cake merits serious consideration. Being fatless, it eliminates a large number of 'heavy' calories. It is a perfect base for summer fruits and trifles as it accommodatingly soaks up fruit juices, flavourings and alcohol. An electric mixer saves time and effort, but it is important to warm the bowl and beaters before whisking begins. It is likewise desirable that ingredients should be at room temperature, especially the eggs. Best results are obtained if the flour and sugar are slightly warmed (see method).

75 g (3 oz) plain flour
75 g (3 oz) caster sugar
3 eggs, size 3

Use a 20.5-cm (8-in) sandwich tin, non-stick preferably, and line the base with a circle of greaseproof paper. *Lightly* brush the tin and the paper with oil. Sift the flour on to a plate or square of foil and leave it on the warmest part of the cooker top. Warm the sugar in the oven for 2–3 minutes. Put the eggs and sugar into the mixing bowl and whisk together steadily until the mixture is pale, fluffy and very thick, leaving a trail around the whisk. (For a hand-whisked sponge, use a wide mixing bowl which fits comfortably into the rim of a saucepan, quarter filled with very hot water. The water must not touch the bottom of the bowl. Place the bowl in the saucepan over a very low heat and do not allow the water to boil.) This takes about 10 minutes of hand-whisking using a fine wire whisk, and 5 minutes with an electric mixer.

Remove the bowl from the saucepan and whisk for another minute or two to cool the mixture. Sieve the flour on to the surface of the whisked foam and, using a metal spoon, lightly cut and fold in the flour thoroughly but quickly, so that the air is not expelled. Folding is complete when every speck of flour has disappeared. Pour the mixture into the prepared tin. Place in the centre of the oven at 180°C (350°F) mark 4 and bake for 20 minutes. Leave to cool in the tin for a few minutes. Run a palette knife around the edge of the tin to loosen the sides. Turn on to a wire rack and allow to cool. Slice the cake in half horizontally, giving two layers.

This sponge keeps for 2 days, covered in foil in an airtight container. It freezes well and is a useful standby for unexpected entertaining.

900 calories for the sponge

Fillings

Where cream is used in these fillings, use really cold whipping cream and lighten this by folding in stiffly beaten egg white:

170-ml (6-oz) carton whipping cream
1 large egg white
5 ml (1 tsp) caster sugar

Whisk the cream until it is thick and will stand in soft peaks. Put the egg white and sugar in a medium size bowl and whip together until stiff. Then lightly fold into the whipped cream. Cover with foil and leave in the refrigerator. This cream will keep for 2–3 days.

650 calories for the cream recipe

Raspberry cream filling
Sprinkle 350 g (12 oz) fresh or frozen raspberries with orange juice or 15 ml (1 tbsp) orange-based liqueur. If necessary, sweeten with 5 ml (1 level tsp) fruit sugar. Mix half the cream with some of the raspberries and fill the centre of the cake. Serve the rest of the fruit and cream separately. Or mix all the fruit and cream together and coat the whole cake.

820 calories for the filling

Summer fruit filling
Use the 170 ml (6 oz) lightened whipped cream mixed with 30 ml (2 tbsp) natural yogurt.

Fill the cake with half the cream and 100 g (4 oz) summer fruits. Spread the remaining cream on top and decorate with another 100 g (4 oz) fruit. This filling may be sweetened with 5 ml (1 level tsp) fruit sugar.

740 calories for the filling

Pineapple, orange and rum filling

Mix the juice of a medium size orange with 15 ml (1 tbsp) dark rum and 15 ml (1 tbsp) pineapple juice from a 227–g (8-oz) can of pineapple rings in natural juice. Spoon half of this liquid over the cake halves and sprinkle the rest over the drained chopped pineapple. Mix the flavoured pineapple flesh into 170 ml (6 oz) lightened whipped cream and pile on to the bottom cake layer. If you want to stretch the cake, use the other half in exactly the same way.

860 calories for the filling

Custard fruit filling

Moisten the cake with 100 ml (4 fl oz) sweet white wine and fill the centre with half quantity of 'Leanline' confectioner's custard (see page 106). Cover with a layer of lightly crushed berries, about 175 g (6 oz), and then the top half of the cake.

415 calories for the filling

The 'leanest' filling

Lightly crush 350 g (12 oz) raspberries and mix with a 141-g (5-oz) carton natural yogurt. Flavour with finely grated orange or lemon peel. Sweeten with 15 g ($\frac{1}{2}$ oz) fruit sugar.

210 calories for the filling

This fatless sponge (900 calories) will serve 8 generously, therefore with, for example, raspberry cream filling (820 calories) the calories will work out at 215 per slice.

Lean spicy fruit cake

225 g (8 oz) self-raising wholemeal
   flour
15 g ($\frac{1}{2}$ oz) porridge oats
5 ml (1 level tsp) baking powder
2.5 ml ($\frac{1}{2}$ level tsp) mixed spice
2.5 ml ($\frac{1}{2}$ level tsp) cinnamon
1.25 ml ($\frac{1}{4}$ level tsp) nutmeg
75 g (3 oz) soft dark brown sugar
75 g (3 oz) low fat spread

2 eggs, size 3
scant 150 ml ($\frac{1}{4}$ pint) skimmed milk
15 ml (1 tbsp) black treacle
175 g (6 oz) cooked drained prunes,
   weighed after cooking with the
   stones in
50 g (2 oz) currants
25 g (1 oz) raisins

In a large bowl, mix together the flour, oats, baking powder, spices and sugar. Rub in the fat which should be used straight from the refrigerator. Lightly beat the eggs with half the milk. Stir in the treacle and beat again.

Scissor the drained prunes into quarters, lifting out the stones at the same time. Stir into the flour mixture then add the remaining fruit. Tip in the egg and milk mixture and gently stir with a wooden spoon or use the low speed on an electric beater to blend all the ingredients. You may need a little of the remaining milk as the mixture should be fairly wet and soft.

Pour the cake mixture into an 18-cm (7-in) non-stick cake tin or one lined with non-stick paper. Alternatively, when using an ordinary cake tin, place a circle of greaseproof paper on the base and lightly brush oil over the paper and sides. Use the minimum amount of oil – too much will make the cake surface soggy and add unnecessary calories!

Bake in the oven, one shelf below centre, starting at 180°C (350°F) mark 4 for 30 minutes, reducing the heat to 170°C (325°F) mark 3 for 50–60 minutes. Check after 1 hour 20 minutes as the cake is better when it is not overcooked. Cool for a few minutes in the tin before turning out on to a wire rack. This cake improves if allowed to store for 24 hours before eating and is even better after 2 days.

The final weight of this cake varies slightly but should be about 850 g (1 lb 14 oz)
145 calories per 50-g (2-oz) slice

Lean date and cherry fruit cake

Illustrated in colour facing page 93

225 g (8 oz) self-raising wholemeal flour	175 g (6 oz) dates
1.25 ml ($\frac{1}{4}$ level tsp) nutmeg	50 g (2 oz) glacé cherries
2.5 ml ($\frac{1}{2}$ level tsp) cinnamon	100 g (4 oz) currants
25 g (1 oz) fruit sugar	100 g (4 oz) low fat spread
50 g (2 oz) soft dark brown sugar	2 eggs, size 3
	scant 150 ml ($\frac{1}{4}$ pint) skimmed milk

In a large bowl, mix together the flour, spices and sugars. Wash the dates thoroughly, dry on kitchen paper and chop. Rinse the cherries in warm water, dry thoroughly and cut into quarters. Add the dates, cherries and currants to the dry ingredients. Make a well in the centre and add the fat straight from the refrigerator, eggs and milk. Beat for 2–3 minutes,

preferably with an electric beater, until the mixture is smooth. Spoon into a lightly oiled 18-cm (7-in) cake tin.

Bake in the oven, one shelf from the bottom, starting at 170°C (325°F) mark 3 for 30 minutes. Reduce the heat to 150°C (300°F) mark 2 for 1 hour and then reduce the heat to 140°C (275°F) mark 1 for the final 20 minutes.

Leave the cake to cool in the tin for 5 minutes before turning out on to a wire rack.

The cake weighs slightly over 900 g (2 lb)
150 calories per 50-g (2-oz) slice

Banana bran fruit cake

This is a moist well flavoured cake that keeps well. It does not need to be thickly buttered although a little honey is very popular.

125 g (4 oz) All-Bran
50 g (2 oz) demerara sugar
50 g (2 oz) currants
50 g (2 oz) dried apricots, soaked and cooked for 5 minutes
5 ml (1 tsp) black treacle

300 ml ($\frac{1}{2}$ pint) skimmed milk
1 175-g (6-oz) ripe banana, weighed with skin
75 g (3 oz) self-raising wholemeal flour
2.5 ml ($\frac{1}{2}$ level tsp) baking powder
2.5 ml ($\frac{1}{2}$ level tsp) mixed spice

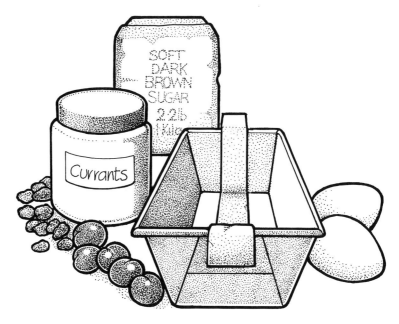

A strip of non-stick paper overhanging the ends of the loaf tin ensures
that a baked cake can be lifted out easily

Put the All-Bran, sugar, currants and well-dried apricots, snipped into strips, in a large bowl. Mix the treacle with the milk, pour this over the bran mixture. Leave to soak for about 30 minutes until the liquid has been taken up by the bran mixture. Peel, mash and work in the banana. Mix the flour with the baking powder and mixed spice. Work the flour into the wet ingredients, stirring until every speck has disappeared.

If possible use a non-stick 450-g (1-lb) loaf tin with a strip of non-stick paper to line the base. Bake in the centre of the oven at 180°C (350°F) mark 4 for 1 hour. Allow to cool for a few minutes before turning out on to a wire rack.

The total calorie count for the whole cake is remarkably low – 1240 calories
Cut into 10 thick slices – 125 calories per slice

'Leanline' sticky fruit cake

Illustrated in colour facing page 93

I find it quite impossible to give up the pleasure of eating cake, especially the sticky kind. This recipe tastes good, keeps well, does not have the disastrous calorie count of usual fruit cakes and it is a great favourite.

100 g (4 oz) **All-Bran**	5 ml (1 tsp) **black treacle**
50 g (2 oz) **soft brown sugar**	300 ml ($\frac{1}{2}$ pint) **skimmed milk**
50 g (2 oz) **dried apricots**	75 g (3 oz) **self-raising wholemeal**
25 g (1 oz) **dried figs**	**flour**
50 g (2 oz) **dried prunes**	2.5 ml ($\frac{1}{2}$ level tsp) **baking powder**
25 g (1 oz) **currants**	2.5 ml ($\frac{1}{2}$ level tsp) **mixed spice**

Place the All-Bran and sugar in a large bowl. Wash the apricots and figs. Dry on kitchen paper and snip into small pieces. Soak the prunes in hot water for a few minutes to soften and scissor-snip the flesh into strips. Add the chopped fruits and currants to the bran and sugar. Mix the treacle into the milk and stir into the bran and fruit mixture. Leave to soak for 30 minutes or until all the liquid has been absorbed.

Mix the flour, baking powder and mixed spice together. Work into the soaked ingredients, stirring until every speck has disappeared. If possible, use a non-stick 450-g (1-lb) loaf tin or an 18-cm (7-in) round cake tin. If using an ordinary tin, line the base with a circle of greaseproof paper and lightly oil the base and sides. Even a non-stick pan needs a light brushing with oil.

Bake in the centre of the oven at 180°C (350°F) mark 4 for 1 hour. Allow to cool for a few minutes before turning out on to a wire rack. When quite cold, store in an airtight container. This cake keeps for up to a week – in fact it improves with keeping – and it freezes well.

105 calories per 50-g (2-oz) slice

Bread

People rarely consider bread as part of a slimming diet. They eat slimmers' bread, rolls and crispbreads, but once these are spread with butter, cheese etc, it is likely that calorie consumption is about the same, especially as the tendency is to eat two slimmers' slices, instead of one slice of ordinary bread. In fact, bread substitutes, weight for weight, contain about the same number of calories as real bread.

Home made bread is a source of temptation, so bake your bread when you are least hungry, straight after a meal, to help to avoid over-indulgence! Alternatively, make small bread rolls weighing about 25 g (1 oz) each. This recipe includes a little *strong* white bread flour, which lightens the bread and lengthens its storage life. Fresh yeast, wrapped in a polythene bag, has a refrigerator life of 2 weeks. It will be destroyed by too much heat, so it is important that the water to be added should be *tepid*.

350 g (12 oz) 100% wholemeal flour
100 g (4 oz) strong white plain flour
7.5 ml (1½ level tsp) salt

15 g (½ oz) fresh yeast
about 350 ml (11–12 fl oz) tepid
water (see method)

Mix the flours and salt together in a large warmed bowl. Put the yeast in a cup, add 15 ml (1 tbsp) tepid water and blend to a cream. Make a well in the flour and pour in the creamed yeast. Then pour in just over 300 ml (½ pint) tepid water and work it into the flour, using a large wooden spoon. If the mixture looks dry and crumbly, add a little more tepid water. Should the mixture be too wet, sprinkle in a little more wholemeal flour. With lightly floured hands, knead the dough for a few minutes until it feels supple and smooth. Sprinkle the dough with a very little flour and cover the bowl with a sheet of polythene, cling film or a tea towel. Do not place the bowl on a boiler or over a heated cooker. Gentle rising produces far better bread. Overheated dough will become dry on the outside and a poor loaf will result.

In an average kitchen temperature, the dough will rise to twice its original size in about 1–2 hours. It really does depend on the warmth of the room. It may suit you to delay the rising process, in which case leave the dough, covered, in a cold room. Return the dough to a warm area and the rising process will resume. Now turn the dough on to a floured board and punch it all over with your fists, flattening the dough to knock out the air bubbles. Knead quickly for 2–3 minutes until the dough feels smooth and springy. Shape the dough into a lightly oiled 900-g (2-lb) loaf tin, tucking the folds underneath. Cover with a cloth and leave it in a warm kitchen. The dough will double in size or fill the tin in about 30–45 minutes.

Bake the loaf in the centre of the oven at 220°C (425°F) mark 7. After 15 minutes reduce the heat to 200°C (400°F) mark 6 and bake for a further 20 minutes. Turn the loaf on to a wire rack. The fully baked loaf will sound hollow when tapped underneath with the knuckles. Cool the bread completely before it is wrapped. I use a tea towel for the first day or two and a polythene bag subsequently.

Rolls

Roll or flatten the dough to a thickness of approximately 2 cm ($\frac{3}{4}$ in). Cut the rolls out with 5-cm (2-in) plain pastry cutter. Place on a lightly oiled baking sheet and leave to rise for 25–30 minutes. Bake in the centre of the oven at 220°C (425°F) mark 7 for 12–15 minutes. Cool on a wire rack.

To freeze Freeze as soon as they have completely cooled, wrapped singly in freezer foil. Crusty rolls have a very limited storage life, therefore bake rolls for the freezer for 12 minutes only and follow the directions below when you want to serve them.

To thaw Leave wrapped at room temperature for $1\frac{1}{2}$ hours. Place, unwrapped, in the oven 200°C (400°F) mark 6 for 5–10 minutes.
   Unthawed rolls should be placed, wrapped, in the oven at 220°C (425°F) mark 7 for 15 minutes.

---

70 calories per 25 g (1 oz) bread

Useful calorie counts
15 g ($\frac{1}{2}$ oz) butter – 113 calories
15 g ($\frac{1}{2}$ oz) honey – 40 calories
15 g ($\frac{1}{2}$ oz) marmalade – 37 calories

'Leanline' menus for feeding the family

Hot soup is a comforting and economical starter. Acquire the habit of making it in advance and store in the fridge or freezer.

———

Soup of choice

Baked mackerel with rosemary (*page 47*)
Braised leeks (*page 82*)
'Leanline' baked potato halves (*page 86*)

Apple and date meringue (*page 96*)

———

Soup

Family meat sauce (*page 56*) with Lemony cabbage (*page 87*)
as a base instead of spaghetti
(spaghetti for the 'lean' members of the family!)

Lean apple purée (*page 98*) with
'Leanline' confectioner's custard (*page 106*)

———

Soup

Rosemary roasted chicken (*page 76*)
'Leanline' red cabbage (*page 87*)
Brown rice (*page 94*)

Raspberry whip (*page 100*)

———

Fish balls (*page 42*)
Salad platter (*page 92*)

Lean lemon cheesecake (*page 104*)

———

Very 'Leanline' beef casserole (*page 58*)
Spiced white cabbage (*page 86*)
Brown rice (*page 94*)

Orange baked bananas with apricots (*page 97*)

———

Mustard marinated chicken (*page 76*)
Leek and swede purée (*page 90*)
'Leanline' baked potato halves (*page 86*)

Rhubarb and orange fool (*page 102*)

———

'Leanline' dinner party menus

Smoked cod's roe mousse (*page 33*)

Spiced leg of lamb (*page 65*)
Leek and swede purée (*page 90*)
'Leanline' baked potato halves (*page 86*)

Luxury lemon cheesecake (*page 103*)

———

Celeriac soup (*page 21*)

Beef braised in white wine (*page 57*)
Brown rice (*page 94*)
Lemony cabbage (*page 87*)

Blackberry and port mousse (*page 99*)

———

Herby cheese starter (*page 30*)

'Leanline' boneless roast loin of pork (*page 67*)
Wine-braised red cabbage (*page 88*)

Apple, apricot and prune party pudding (*page 97*)

———

Stuffed tomatoes (*page 37*)

Plaice fillets in a wine and mushroom sauce (*page 44*)
Courgettes with leeks (*page 84*)
Carrots in chicken stock (*page 91*)
Boiled or steamed new potatoes (*page 85*)

Apricot cheesecake (*page 105*)

———

'Leanline' kipper pâté (*page 32*)

Pork parcels (*page 66*)
Stirred mushrooms (*page 83*) and/or 'Leanline' ratatouille (*page 84*)
Brown rice (*page 94*)

Minted gooseberry mousse (*page 99*)

———

Jerusalem artichoke soup (*page 22*)

Boned apricot chicken (*page 73*)
A green vegetable in season makes a perfect contrast
– French beans, calabrese or broccoli,
lightly cooked in boiling salted water.
Rice

'Leanline' fatless sponge
with raspberry cream or pineapple,
orange and rum filling (*page 108*)

Index